A Child is Missing

Searching for Justice

A true story about the
kidnapping and murder of
13-year-old Kathy Lynn Gloddy
and the family's search for answers

KAREN BEAUDIN

FOREWORD BY
PAMELA J. PETRILLO
Special Investigator

A Child is Missing: A True Story – 2nd ed.
Karen Beaudin
www.KarenBeaudin.com

Cover Design by AlyBlue Media
Interior Design by AlyBlue Media LLC
Published by AlyBlue Media, LLC

ISBN: 978-1944328900
Library of Congress Control Number: 2017917029
AlyBlue Media, LLC
Ferndale, WA 98248
www.AlyBlueMedia.com

PRINTED IN THE UNITED STATES OF AMERICA

Testimonials

"TRUTH... A Child Is Missing emphasizes that there are multiple victims in crimes, and its effects last a lifetime for all involved. I commend the family for standing together and fighting for the truth. By the grace of God, may the truth be told." —RETIRED DET. JAMES A. CONRAD, New Hampshire State Police

"HOPE... The story of the Gloddy family illustrates that the damage caused by murder extends far beyond a young girl whose life was cut short. At the same time, her family has turned tragedy into hope by championing the creation of a Cold Case Homicide Unit in the State of New Hampshire. Hopefully through their efforts, killers who have not been apprehended may still be brought to justice." —N. WILLIAM DELKER, New Hampshire Senior Assistant Attorney General, Homicide Unit and SGT. SCOTT GILBERT, New Hampshire State Police Major Crime Unit, Lead Investigator

"VITAL... A Child Is Missing is an important reminder that some wounds are just too deep, some scars can never heal. Too often, victims are forgotten in the criminal justice system and the media. A Child Is Missing is a painful yet vital glimpse of a murder investigation seen through the eyes of a sister who is still searching for the truth. For anyone who cares about justice beyond the courtroom, this is a must-read." —BOB WARD, Crime Reporter, Fox 25 News, Boston

"POWERFUL... Karen Beaudin has written a powerful and compelling true crime story that originally impacted her small-town American family back in 1971. From the perspective of a loving older sister, Karen offers a personal account of how the still-unsolved brutal murder of her thirteen-year-old sister affected her entire family as the years passed. She painfully recounts how the horrible ordeal shook her core beliefs about humanity. She reveals how she came to cope with the loss of her sister, and offers a path of inspiration for others afflicted with similar pain." —CHIEF THOMAS P. SHAMSHAK (Retired), Shamshak Investigative Services, Inc., Boston, MA

"REMARKABLE... A Child is Missing offers firsthand insight into a family's fight for truth and justice. Although heartbreaking, Karen's candid look into the journey behind the veil offers an education like none other. Truly remarkable." -LYNDA CHELDELIN FELL, International Grief Institute

Contents

Dedication

To my sister Kathy, whose life was brutally taken at the tender age of thirteen. I will never understand how someone could have taken your life in such a horrific way and deny all of us the joy of seeing this magnificent butterfly take flight.

To my mom and dad, who endured the endless pain of never experiencing Kathy's laugh or touch beyond the age of thirteen. Instead of bathing in the warmth of their youngest daughter, they suffered in the knowledge of her brutal death until the day they died.

To my siblings, who experienced with me the pain of losing a sister to the hands of a murderer. We stood together as we faced the image of her brutal death and the destruction it caused to our family. A special mention to my sister Janet; hand in hand we walked through a very dark time.

KAREN BEAUDIN

A CHILD IS MISSING

.

BY PAMELA J. PETRILLO

Foreword

"I've tried to remember what she was wearing, but can't. Why didn't anyone ask questions about what had happened? This isn't some story or movie you're writing about. This is real. We are people who are suffering."

These are the heartbroken words that documented a life forever changed by the abduction, rape, and murder of an innocent girl. Even after these heinous actions, those who loved her most can only hope the child suffered not in death, as the mad man ran over her again and again with his car, insuring she never told his tale. A beautiful young girl transfixed in time by the brutal savage who took her life—and her tender, suffering sister who could never let her go—together weave for us this true story of unspeakable tragedy. Together, one lost and one alive, Karen Beaudin manages to find hope in the emptiness. For all fellow travelers who need a guide in chaos, this moving story reminds us of the steel woven into the fabric of our lives in spite of the evil of mankind. The human spirit can still surprise us with its endless tenacity in facing what is beyond compare. God still holds those who endure it in the living cradle of His arms.

You will be riveted to the pages of this sorrowful story, and fascinated with the endurance this family exhibits as they face the lives and deaths of those they love most. May God give them the peace and resolution they so richly deserve. Who will be the one that brings this murderer his due? Who will find the ultimate answer for those waiting so long? Who will bring the little sparrow to her final resting place, as the last chapter of this innocent young girl's life unfolds within this saga? Will he finally be caught? Be the prayer warrior who makes it so as you share in the lives and deaths of this precious family as they let us see within their sorrow. May justice rightly be served!

PAMELA J. PETRILLO
Special Investigator

CHAPTER ONE

She walked by my window. She wasn't smiling, but she seemed to be telling me she was all right and not to worry about her. Her look of contentment told me that even though I couldn't change what had happened to her, she wasn't sad. Over the years I've tried to remember what she was wearing, but I can't. I don't know why that mattered, but it did—or seemed to.

I slept by a window in the room we shared. I was looking through this window when I saw her walking by, graceful and confident. As she passed by my window, I noticed the yellow flowers were in bloom on the forsythia bush. How could they be in bloom? It was cold outside, and the month was November.

My eyes flew open; I sat up in bed and called out her name, "Kathy! Kathy!" I looked through the window, hoping to see her but starting to realize it was a dream. It was dark out, and she was nowhere to be found. I pressed my face against the window and searched for her. My heart ached to see her again. I stared intently, thinking that if I waited long enough she would appear, but she never did. Trying to fall back to sleep, I prayed for the dream to return so I could see her. I finally fell asleep, but the dream did not return—not that night nor any other night in the future.

Night after night, I would visualize it again, step by step. As I fell asleep, I hoped I could bring the dream back, bring her back to let her know how much I loved her and how terribly I missed her. The room we shared seemed so empty without her. Every night I saw the bed she slept in and knew the clothes she wore were still in her bureau, never to be worn by her again. No one wanted to disturb her belongings in the hope she might return; but of course, she never did.

CHAPTER TWO

The night Kathy went missing was not an ordinary night. Usually I watched the little boys across the street, but I was attending my high school sports banquet, so my sister Janet was watching them until I returned home. After the banquet, I stopped home first. When I entered the house, my mom told me that my younger sister, Kathy, left earlier to go to Bell's Variety store and wasn't home yet. I could see the anxiety on her face.

I reassured her, saying, "Mom, don't worry. I'm sure she's okay." I did think it strange she was not home. It was not like her to be out alone at such a late hour, but I was sure there wasn't anything to worry about. I went to the house across the street and finished watching the children until their parents returned.

In our small, quiet town, walking alone was never a cause for concern. Kathy was in eighth grade, and I was a sophomore in high school. We repeatedly walked to and from school, and walking by ourselves to the little store near our home was not unusual. If we wanted to go downtown, we walked. We walked everywhere, and we always felt safe in our little town. We never felt that crime and evil were lurking around every corner. It was a safe town in which to raise a family. Neighbors knew neighbors, and neighborhood children played with neighborhood children.

As I sat in the living room waiting for the little boys' parents to return, something peculiar happened. Kathy's German shepherd dog, Tasha, came to the front door and wanted to be let inside. Boy, did she want to come in! She was jumping on the door, scratching like crazy. "Okay, okay," I said and let her in.

None of us gave Tasha much attention; she was Kathy's dog, and it was unusual for her to visit me while I was at that house. She came inside and began what I later realized was a search. She sniffed every corner of the downstairs and then continued her frantic search upstairs. Back downstairs and panting uncontrollably, she lay down and just looked at me. I looked back at her, thinking how crazy she was acting.

"What is wrong with you?" I asked. She knew something wasn't right. Something had happened to her master: the young girl who loved and cared for her. She lay there for a short time and then ran for the front door to be let outside. She jumped on the door, clawing at it as if she was desperate to be free. Exasperated, I ran over and said, "Okay, you crazy dog. I'll let you out." Off she went to continue her search, and I closed the door.

Around 11:30 p.m. I returned home and saw my mom sitting in the chair in our living room. Janet was with her, and I could see the strain on her face. She said, "Kathy's still not home. We've called the police." She told me the police said they would look for her walking on the streets, but there was nothing they could do until she had been missing for twenty-four hours. "Not to worry," they said. "Kids run away all the time, and she'll probably show up soon." I'll never forget Mom's expression as she began to cry and said, "Something terrible has happened."

I've heard stories about mother's intuition. They can sense when their children are in danger or when something just isn't right, but they can't put their finger on it. She knew in her heart Kathy was in trouble, that something was terribly wrong. We tried to comfort her, to reassure her that there must be some explanation; although, at this point we couldn't imagine what that might be. It was not like Kathy to leave at night, to not tell anyone where she was. I slowly began to realize that my mom was right. Something was terribly wrong.

I'm not exactly sure what time my dad arrived home that night, but when he did, he and I set out in the car looking for her. Janet stayed with my mom so she wouldn't be alone. Dad drove, and I kept my eyes on the sidewalks, looking for a young girl walking. My eyes carefully scanned both sides of the road as he drove along.

It wasn't as though we had a certain direction we thought she might be going, so we just drove. I mentioned that some friends of hers lived nearby, and we headed that way. Even though it was late, I knocked on the door to ask if anyone had seen her. No one had. Then we drove by the high school, my eyes still searching for any sign of her. We went across the river and past the road that led to the small ski area in Franklin. I looked up that road and felt strongly that we should go up there. It was a powerful tug in my heart, but I dismissed it as silly. Why would she be up there? We should stick to the main roads; if we were to see her walking, it would be there.

Later I regretted not telling my dad to drive up that road. Would it have made a difference? Probably not; but just the same, I did regret not listening to what my heart was telling me. We went farther up the road and finally decided to go home. We hoped she would be there and all would be well. We pulled into the driveway, and I thought to myself, If Kathy isn't with us, Mom's hopes will be dashed. She would see we had failed at our mission to bring her home.

We walked through the front door, and I knew by the look on my mom's face that Kathy had not returned. Mom looked to us with hope, and when her little girl didn't come around the corner, she sank in her chair, and the tears in her eyes told me she still feared the worst. Even though I could not figure out where Kathy had gone and why she wasn't home, I still believed that at any time she would walk through the door, or the phone would ring and her voice would be on the other end. She would give us some excuse as to why she wasn't home, and all would be well. But that didn't happen.

CHAPTER THREE

After a sleepless night, morning came but brought no further news of Kathy. The police were again notified that she was still missing. We were very concerned now. They said they would be on the lookout for her, but that we shouldn't worry too much. She probably had run away and would show up soon. We told them it wasn't like her to be gone from home overnight, that we really did feel something was wrong. They still didn't seem concerned, and we felt nothing was going to be done.

Janet and I decided to take matters into our own hands. We began to look for her, starting out at her school, asking questions. We were hoping to talk to someone who might know something.

One of the teachers spoke with a friend of Kathy's to see if she had any information about her disappearance. She returned to tell us that this girl and Kathy were planning to run away together. They were supposed to meet at the Franklin Falls Dam. We were also warned to take what this girl had to say with a "grain of salt" because she had a tendency to make up stories to get attention. At this point, Janet and I were thankful for any information and went to the police station to tell them what we had found out.

We spoke with the chief of police and told him what we knew. One of the officers laughed at us and said, "See, I told you she probably ran away." To us, the situation wasn't funny. We still hadn't found her, and we didn't know if this girl was telling the truth. Our concern was not with the running away part; it was in finding her. It was a relief to think that we would be bringing her home soon.

Janet and I jumped into the police cruiser to help look for her at the dam. When we got there, we all began calling her name and searching the area. I screamed at the top of my lungs, "Kathy, Kathy, where are you? This is not funny; you better answer me. We're not mad. Please just answer."

There was no voice calling back, "I'm over here!" No one saying, "I'm so sorry I made you all worry about me." My heart sank as I realized we had been given false information and that the girl had indeed lied. Kathy wasn't here; she was still missing.

Things were getting serious now, and surely the police would get more involved. They seemed to carry on with no urgency. The fact that she was not at the dam really brought about a sinking feeling within my heart. She just wouldn't leave the house like that and not return without a word, without a phone call. Something was definitely wrong. My heart was sending me a message of fear, but my head kept telling me that there must be some explanation.

What's the next step? Where do we go from here? Who can we call? Where can we look? There has to be something I can do. Think, Karen. Where would you go? Even if I had thought to run away, I don't know where I would have gone. I had no answers, just a bunch of questions. I decided to look around the neighborhood again and headed down to the railroad tracks near our home. Sometimes we went that way because it was a shortcut to and from school and the store. As I walked the railroad tracks, I looked around to see if there was anything unfamiliar—an item on the ground, perhaps, something she might have dropped while she was on her journey.

I'm not sure how long I had been gone, but after some time I decided to head home with hope that she would be there, that as I walked through the front door, she would be standing there. First, I would be thankful she was okay and finally home. Then I would be angry with her because she had worried us so. I thought, I'm going to tell her that I don't care what her excuse is; she had better not ever do this again. I'm going to tell her how much I love her and that I was just terrified thinking something awful had happened to her; all of us were.

As I walked into the house, the scene I beheld was like something out of a movie. Police were there. Why would the police be here? My mom was sitting in the same chair as the night before, and Janet was on the edge of it with her arms around her. Everyone was crying; the doctor had a syringe with a needle at the end, and I watched as he placed it into my mother's arm. Janet sat there sobbing. As my eyes scanned around the room, I saw the police, our family doctor, my grandmother, Janet, and my dad.

I looked at everyone and said, "What's wrong? What's the matter?" Every eye turned toward me but no one spoke a word. I said again, "What's wrong? Why is everyone crying?"

As tears ran down my sister's face, she said with a voice filled with sobs, "Kathy's dead; she's been murdered."

I stared at her with disbelief and tried to absorb each word she had spoken. One by one, each word ran through my head slowly and deliberately. "Kathy's dead; she's been murdered." I stood there as if frozen in time. I couldn't move. I will never forget the look on Janet's face as she told me they had found Kathy. She was dead—murdered—and she was never coming back home to be with us again.

I just stood there saying over and over again, "No, you're wrong. There must be some mistake. No, that can't be. You're wrong." Everyone was looking at me as I tried to comprehend the words that had come out of my sister's mouth. Then our eyes locked, and as I watched the tears fall down her face, I realized what she had told me was true.

I walked away into the kitchen and put my face into a corner and sobbed. No, I thought, this cannot be happening. Not in this little town; not to our family. So there I stood in a corner, not wanting to face anyone, just wanting to disappear into the walls, to go to a place where all of this would go away and when I walked out on the other side, all would be well.

My grandmother came into the kitchen and approached me with a look of disapproval on her face. "Stop your crying! Your mother can hear you. Do you want to upset her even more than she already is?"

I had just found out that my little sister had been taken from us forever, and she was telling me to stop crying.

As I tried to muffle my cries of sorrow, someone knocked on the door. It was a boy I knew well because we both competed on the local swim team. His dad was a doctor in the community; and even though they might be considered in a different class than my family, they never acted as if they were better than anyone else.

As I turned to look at him, he said, "Karen, I heard Kathy is missing. I can take my minibike out to the bluffs and look for her." The bluffs were a place where the neighborhood kids would hang out. It was like having a secret treehouse of sorts, just a wooded area where all of us would go. My heart was thankful that he cared enough to stop by and see if there was anything he could do.

I stood there and stared at him, not knowing what to say. My grandmother turned my way and said, "I'll take care of this" and then proceeded to walk outside with him. I wondered what she would tell him. Would she be kind? After the scolding she gave me, I hoped she would be gentle in telling him the news we had just received.

For God hath not given us the spirit of fear: but
of power, and of love, and of a sound mind

II Timothy 1:7 KJV

CHAPTER FOUR

Some of the events following the devastating news of Kathy's death are so clear and vivid; others are muted in gray. I started going through the motions, doing what was supposed to be done, but I couldn't always remember why I was there and for what purpose. People would talk to me, hug me, and say how sorry they were, but I couldn't unscramble the words that came out from their lips. Other things were so clear that no matter how much time would go by, I would remember every emotion and see every detail.

The phone kept ringing. Journalists called for interviews. Family and friends also called, wanting to know if it was true. We finally took the phone off the receiver. It was all so overwhelming. Police were everywhere in the house—detectives asking questions and looking through her things for something that might give them a clue to what had happened and with whom she had been that night.

We endured these things for months and months, and it seemed it would never end. On top of preparing for a funeral for my sister, who was just thirteen, we had to be interrogated with question after question. One question asked of me was, "Do you know anyone who would do this to your sister?"

I looked at him and thought, Who would do such a thing? How would I know anyone who would even contemplate such an evil thing? Who would take a life in such a brutal way? Of course I don't know who would do this! I looked into his unsympathetic eyes, unemotional and focused on the task at hand, and answered, "No."

My family began planning for the horrible day when we would have to face the reality of saying goodbye and placing Kathy in the ground. Since it was November, we were told by the groundskeeper of the cemetery that we would have to wait until spring to have the burial because the ground had already started to freeze.

That news was crushing. None of us wanted to go through that. The thought of having a funeral and then reliving it all in the spring was more than any one of us could bear. Because of the circumstances, the groundskeeper changed his mind, and we were going to be allowed to have the burial. Kathy would be put in the ground that cold November in 1971.

As the investigation continued, it revealed more and more about what had happened to Kathy and the way she died. We found out that she was seen by a neighborhood boy on her way to the store near our house. They waved to each other and said hi. She got to the store and bought a couple of items to eat: potato sticks and an ice cream sandwich. Potato sticks were one of her favorite snacks.

After leaving the store, she walked to the high school, where I was attending the sports banquet. The cafeteria was on the basement level, and a girl who knew Kathy noticed her looking in the window. She waved at Kathy and then saw her look diagonally across the lawn. She then observed Kathy walking toward the driveway until she was out of sight. Kathy headed toward the bridge just beyond the high school, and that is where she was last seen.

Through the questioning of the investigators, we began to hear exactly how she was found and details of some of the things done to her. The facts trickled out one by one. I knew she had been murdered, but never in my wildest imagination would I have guessed all that was going to be revealed to us.

How she was murdered was horrific and brutal. It wasn't enough to repeatedly rape her, but she was also beaten, strangled, and run over by a car multiple times. The murderer wanted to make sure she was dead because he didn't want to be caught, which revealed the obvious: she knew who he was. As if that wasn't enough, he left her completely naked in the woods except for the socks she was wearing.

The sorrow of knowing these things was like a hand upon my heart, squeezing until the pressure became so great that I felt the life within me slowly drifting away. I felt physical pain in my heart, a hurt so intense I literally thought I might have a heart attack.

If this was how I felt, I couldn't even imagine what my parents were going through. What was their pain like? Surely it had to be worse than mine; she was their little girl, the baby in the family. But how could their pain be worse? Could a person really survive more pain than what I was feeling? It was unimaginable. How does a person process and understand that life will go on or that the pain could ever get easier? All I could think was, please, God, make this pain go away.

CHAPTER FIVE

My sister and brothers came home once again. The reunion was not a joyful one. Ann was the oldest in the family, followed by the twins, Richard and Roger. Janet was next in line, then me, and lastly Kathy. Ann came from Rochester, New Hampshire. Mom and Kathy had recently gone to see Ann and her new baby, Jennifer. Ann would cherish that memory and the hug Kathy gave her as they were leaving, not realizing it would be the last time she would ever see her.

Richard flew in from Pennsylvania, and Roger from Germany. Roger was in the military and was serving his country at the time of Kathy's death. He had a long flight to take, and I imagined the hours on the plane thinking about what had happened were grueling.

At the time of Kathy's death, Janet and I still lived at home. We would be the ones left behind to speak with police and detectives on a regular basis and try to pick up the pieces. The pain was deep for all of us, but the future would reveal things to Janet and I that no two sisters should have to see or talk about.

I had just turned fifteen in October, and by November, I realized that my thirteen-year-old sister would never graduate, have a career, get married, or have children. She would never have the opportunity to give to the world what she possessed inside: love and kindness.

A friend of mine once told Kathy about a little purse that she liked in a store on Main Street. Kathy ran down to the store and purchased it for her. As my friend and I stood in the driveway, Kathy came walking up with the purse in her hand and presented it to her. I couldn't believe that she ran there, bought the purse, and ran all the way back so she could give it to her before she went home.

That was Kathy—wanting to please others, looking for ways to bring a little sunshine into someone else's life. She offered encouraging words to those who felt down, and she wanted everyone to know they were important. She once told the young girl who lived across the street from us that she wasn't homely in the new glasses she had to wear. Her friend wasn't happy about having glasses, and Kathy wanted her to know that they weren't as bad as she imagined them to be. Kathy didn't look for anything in return. Knowing that she had made someone feel better about him or herself was good enough for her.

She was a tomboy who loved poetry and wrote some poems of her own. She went to St. Mary's school, and after her death, the school started a poetry contest in her honor. I read some of the poems she had written and realized there was an unexplained sadness in them. She seemed so concerned about things I didn't give much thought to.

Her poems were written in the late sixties, and many of them were about the war and not understanding its purpose. She expressed sadness over knowing that men and women were dying while they defended their country. At the age of fifteen, I knew about the war, but it wasn't something I thought a lot about. My concerns were more about my friends, our activities, and cheerleading for our local team. But not Kathy. She was concerned about the war and about the environment, recycling, and wanting to go with her best friend to a clothing drive held by St. Mary's School.

The local paper did an article about the recycling of cans going on in our garage, and a picture of her was included. She would manually crush cans with a brick and then place them in a large garbage bag. I think about the future she might have had. I'm sure it would have been one that would have involved fighting for a cause or for the rights of one who could not fight for him or herself. She would have taken her place in society as a public servant in some way.

When she died, her life was in transition, trying to break out of the tomboy image and into the age of being a young woman. We should have been able to celebrate this transition with her, but instead we began the dismal task of planning her funeral.

As the funeral was being planned, most of the decisions were left up to us, her siblings. Mom and Dad were in such a horrible state that we tried to take care of all funeral plans. One important decision was what she would wear for the funeral. Kathy didn't care to wear dresses, but a dress would be chosen for that day.

Ann and Janet went shopping to pick something out that would be appropriate. They bought a dress that Kathy would have worn if she were to wear a dress—short sleeves, scoop neck, with daisies on it.

Daisies were her favorite flower. Ann and Janet softly said to me, "You'll like it, Karen. It looks like something she would wear."

There was such sweetness in their voices. My approval was important to them, so even though I thought being in jeans and a T-shirt would have been more like her, I knew they had made the right decision. The dress was brought to the funeral home so her body could be prepared for the viewing.

Shortly after the dress was delivered, the phone rang. After the conversation, I saw my sisters crying. They told me it was the funeral director. He remorsefully told us that the dress chosen wasn't appropriate because there was a lot of bruising on Kathy's body. The type of clothing she needed to wear had to be something with a high neck and long sleeves.

As we took in that information, the three of us stood there hugging one another, overwhelmed by the image in our minds. Understanding that someone had hurt our little sister in such a way was horrifying, and the thought of how much she might have suffered before she took her last breath was unbearable. I realized then how cruel this world had become for all of us, and how empty and hollow the future would be without her.

The viewing was the following day, so we had no time to shop for anything else. I decided to bring out a dress I had worn to my eighth grade prom. The neckline was very high with lace around the edge, and the sleeves were long with the same lace trim at the bottom. It wasn't something Kathy would pick out to wear—it was much too fancy—but it was something that would be appropriate. So the decision was made; she was to be buried in the dress I had worn just one year before to my junior high prom. Ann looked at me and said, "Karen, are you sure this is what you want to do?"

"It's okay. I want her to wear it. Knowing she's wearing something of mine is comforting to me. Kind of like my arms are wrapped around her."

So the dress that was used for a night of dancing and for representing my school on the queen's court would now be used to cover my beloved sister as she took her final resting place here on earth inside a casket.

The next morning as we prepared to go to the funeral home, we received a phone call from the funeral director. I could feel the anxiety grow in the room as we waited to hear what the phone call was about.

Lately, whenever the phone rang it wasn't because someone had good news. I stood there in shock as I heard the details of why he was calling. He explained that "they" (whoever they were) had taken Kathy's body to transport it back to the hospital where the autopsy had been performed. He couldn't give us an explanation because he didn't have one. He was notified that they were coming to take her, and that's what they did.

Questions flew around the room like wildfire. Did they miss something during the autopsy? Was there something they forgot to do? Had new evidence come in? And who are they? No one ever called my family to let us know that they were going to remove Kathy's body from the funeral home; they left it up to the funeral director to do it.

The viewing was scheduled for that day, so there must have been a good reason for them to transport her back to the hospital. The viewing was delayed another day.

CHAPTER SIX

The time had finally come. The day of the viewing was here, and I would've given anything not to go through this. It was a sadness I'll never forget. My poor mom and dad. How would they ever bear this?

I didn't want to cry around them, knowing how hard it was to face the reality of the day. I was fifteen but I tried to be an adult. I tried to be strong and help them as much as I could. Ann, Roger, Richard, Janet, and I were involved in all the decisions that needed to be made so our parents didn't have to think about what needed to be done.

As we entered the funeral home, my heart was pounding. A voice screamed inside me saying, "Turn around and run! Don't go in there." I knew once I saw her that reality would set in and there would be no way to pretend she was still alive. The funeral director met us at the door and talked with us before we entered the room where Kathy was. He expressed how sorry he was for our loss and for the tragedy our family was going through. He assured us that he handled Kathy with care and did the best he could.

He said, "If she doesn't look the way you would like, then we still can have a closed casket." This would be the first time any of us would look at Kathy since her murder; and because of what the funeral director told us, I was frightened to go in. I didn't want to see her lying in a casket without life, without the movement of breath going in and out of her lungs; it frightened me to think that I might see signs that she had been hurt. I didn't want to see the bruises, the marks of what he had done to the sister I loved so much.

The family entered the room and had private time with her before anyone else arrived. All of us stood back while our parents approached the casket. They needed time alone with Kathy, so we just waited as they knelt there in front of her. My heart was broken for them. The pain I felt from losing Kathy was intensified seeing the tremendous sorrow they were going through. If there was any way I could have eased their pain, even just a little, I would have done it. It was so hard to see them like that. This was not the way it was supposed to be.

As I made my way toward the casket, I felt my body begin to shake, and I thought I might be sick. Ann walked with me, and together we knelt down in front of her. The young girl in front of me didn't look like my sister. They had used a lot of makeup on her face and hands. Her hair wasn't the way she would have worn it; her bangs swooped across her forehead as if to hide an injury. Even with all that makeup you could still see bruises up near her neck and on her hands. I knew I would always remember the image of her lying there. It wasn't her, and I didn't want people to see her that way.

24

I closed my eyes and tried to picture her running. Even on my best day, I could never beat her. I tried to see her smile and hear her laughter. But nothing. The image of her lying there was already stamped inside my brain, and I would never be able to erase it. As I knelt, I wished I hadn't seen her like that. I wanted a closed casket. I spoke to Ann about my concern with others seeing her like that. But of course, the final decision was my mom's, and she was determined for some reason to have the casket open. I considered that the finality of it all once the casket was closed might be too much for her right now. I didn't understand it all, but I knew that if it made it easier for her, then it was what we needed to do.

I approached her casket a second time by myself; I wanted to have some time alone with her. As I cried, I told her how much I missed her already, that I wished it had been me instead of her. The thought of her suffering was such a burden to bear.

All I knew about God was what I learned from Catholic school and attending mass. I didn't have a personal relationship with Him. Like so many, I called on Him only in a time of need. I understood He went to the cross, but didn't realize it was for me. I began to pray, "Please, God. I pray she didn't suffer, that it was over quickly."

I thought to myself that if God wanted her to live, He would have allowed it. He could raise her from the dead if He wanted to.

I reasoned in my mind that for her to live with what she had been through, the pain of it all would be much harder than death. God knew best, and to be with Him would be better than living with a mind tortured by what had happened to her. Of course, I asked God why something so awful would happen. I realized even at the age of fifteen that it was not God who was the author of evil but man. It's man who turns his back on God and in doing so leads a life filled with deception and self-gratification, not caring about the consequences or the effects it has on another human being.

I don't know how many people came to the viewing that day. The lines seemed to never end. We stood there for hours as people told us how sorry they were for our loss and how it was such a tragedy. I saw people walking by me, but they were just bodies with no faces. Family, friends, teachers, and classmates attended. In the end, no one made an impression on me with their words or actions. No one brought any peace or comfort to me. The one thing that stayed with me was what the funeral director said to us before people started to arrive.

First, he told us that he did the best he could to prepare for the viewing, and then he said, "Please instruct people not to touch her. She is very fragile." What did he mean by that? Images rushed through my mind. I couldn't comprehend exactly what he meant by that. Over and over I rehearsed that sentence in my mind; it just tumbled around and around. What happened to her that would make him say such a thing? How could someone have hurt her so?

We said our final goodbyes that night. Tomorrow would be the funeral. I walked up to the casket, and this time as I looked at her, I began to cry. I closed my eyes and prayed, "Please, God, help me to remember the way she was and not this way. Help me remember her smile, her laugh, her tomboyish ways. She was special, and I didn't realize how much until she was gone."

Realizing how extraordinary she was and that I would never have the chance to see her grow and use her gifts brought sadness to me that was separate from all the rest of the sorrow I was feeling.

Night came, and the pain only worsened. Alone in the room we shared, I laid my head down on my pillow and tried to imagine that she was in her bed next to me sound asleep. Maybe if I closed my eyes I could hear her breathing or hear the sound of movement as she turned. "God, I'm here. Can you hear me? Please make this all go away. When morning comes, make it all a dream. Just a terrible dream ... "

From exhaustion I drifted off to sleep; but when I awoke in the morning, nothing had changed. Kathy wasn't in her bed. She had been brutally murdered, and we still had a funeral to attend. How would we all endure the day, seeing her casket closed and watching as she was slowly lowered into the ground? How do a mother and father cope with losing their daughter in such a brutal way? How do they say their final goodbyes? How does one do that? Nothing in life could prepare us for that. No book to read, no instruction manual. It's a time in life that no one should ever have to walk through.

I would like more sisters, that the taking
out of one, might not leave such stillness.

EMILY DICKINSON
*

CHAPTER SEVEN

The morning was filled with anxiety and a sense of hopelessness. We prepared for what would be the second most trying day of our lives—Kathy's funeral. The first being the day we found out that Kathy had been murdered and that she was never returning home to us again. I went through the motions of getting dressed; each step I took was extremely difficult. How could the small task of getting dressed require so much energy?

Before leaving the house, I looked at the room we shared and knew that it would never be the same. My life, our lives, would be forever changed.

People told me that time would heal my heart, but I didn't believe it. To be totally healed I would need to turn back the hands of time. I would need to enter a place where such an event did not occur. I knew that I would carry the scars from this for the rest of my life. The only way to escape from the pain would be to take my own life, and that was not an option.

We met at the funeral home and were told how the day would go. What order the cars would follow each other to the church and with whom we would ride. We were instructed on what would happen after the graveside ceremony and where we would be taken from there. As I stood outside listening to what was being said, I glanced over my shoulder. There she was in the back of the car, with the casket closed. Was she really in there? Maybe it wasn't her I saw yesterday lying there; it had to be someone else. It just had to be; this could not be happening. But as we were told to get in the cars for the short ride to the church, I knew that it was real; and no matter how hard I wished or prayed, the events of this day were not going to change.

We entered the church building and were guided to the front, where we waited as people filled the pews. When the service began, I sat there staring at her casket. Seeing it there made everything seem final. My mind was racing, and I couldn't make out what was being said. None of it was important to me; none of it would change a thing. As I glanced around the building, I was overwhelmed by how many people had attended the ceremony. Buses transported children from her school. How had her murder affected them? How hard was it for her friends and classmates? How would it change their lives in the future? I knew mine would be changed forever.

As I walked past her casket for the final time and reached out to gently rest my hand on top, I beckoned her to come back. I was willing to give her my beating heart in place of her silent one. I returned to my seat and began to cry, knowing that within me there was no power to give her life. I felt an arm come around me. Looking up, I saw

Richard's face looking at me with compassion. His eyes connected with mine and conveyed "I know the pain is great." His tender eyes told me he loved me and he wished he could take it all away.

After the service, I went down the aisle to the front doors of the church. I couldn't look up. With my head down, I contemplated what was next. The finality of it would hurt. Back outside, I got into the car, and one by one we pulled out into a line and headed to the tiny cemetery in Tilton, where Kathy was to be placed in the ground. As we drove away I turned my head to see the cars behind us. It was an overwhelming sight. There were so many cars following us. Were they here because they loved her or just because they wanted to be part of something horrific that had happened to our sleepy little town? In some ways, I wished they would all go away and leave us alone, but I also knew that others did love and care for her. They needed closure too.

We approached the cemetery. I took a deep breath, bracing myself for what would happen next. Stepping out of the car, I slowly walked to the area that was prepared for her and stood by the grave, shivering in the cold. I was thankful to know that we would not be standing in the same place when spring came, that they allowed us to have the burial now. We were all thankful for that, especially my mom and dad. Going through this stage of the funeral once was more than enough for anyone to cope with. I heard people speaking, but their words went drifting by as if caught up by the wind. There were so many people there. She would be amazed at how many had come to say goodbye. Many of her friends and classmates were there.

My mind went back to her once again. How her murder would affect them. There wouldn't be any counseling for most of them. Whom would they talk to? How would they deal with the emotions of losing a friend or classmate in such a horrible way? Janet and I would not receive counseling either, but we would have each other. I wondered if we would talk about it or if we would keep what we felt inside. I didn't think we should talk to our parents about it because it would be too painful for them.

The ceremony was done, and I began to walk toward the car that brought me. I didn't want to leave her there. I knew that she was gone and that I wouldn't see her again, but I still felt terrible that we were leaving her behind. Walking away was so final. It was the last step in letting her go. Realizing this took my breath away. The thought of her being put into the ground was just too overwhelming for me. I tried to block it out of my mind, telling myself to think of something else, but I couldn't. As I sat in the car with my sisters, tears began to run down my cheeks. We hugged each other, and I wanted to hold on to them forever.

After the ceremony, we gathered with family and friends at a relative's house. I wanted to go home, but I knew that this was what people did after a funeral. People stood around talking and eating. I could hear conversations around the room and picked up on someone laughing. How dare they? How could anyone laugh at a time like this? Would laughter even be a part of life in the future? I sat on the stairs that led to the upper level of the house and closed my eyes. "God, I just want to go home. Why are we here?"

CHAPTER EIGHT

The days following the funeral were filled with phone calls from journalists and news stations hoping for interviews with the family. A reporter from one particular newspaper showed up at the house and asked my dad if he might ask him a few questions. My dad spoke with the man briefly. Dad approached me and said that they wanted to take a picture of me outside our house with the dog that came home without Kathy. I looked at my dad, my eyes pleading with him to make them go away. His eyes were full of sympathy, but he told me to sit on the steps so they could take the picture. He just wanted them gone. So I sat there with my arm around her dog and looked up at the camera.

As I focused in on the person taking the picture, I thought to myself, I hate you. Don't you realize what we are going through? This isn't some story or movie you're writing about. This is real. We are people who are suffering, and it hurts more than we could describe.

Memories of my parents during this time are gray. Janet and I had each other, although we often suffered alone, keeping our emotions to ourselves. We tried to comfort our parents—give them a hug, see if they needed anything—but we didn't talk about what had happened. My parents entered a world that was unreachable, one in which they couldn't be comforted. We understood that, and we didn't ask for anything from them in return for the love we gave them. We knew that we probably shouldn't expect much from them for years to come. How could we? Their child was no longer missing; she had been brutally raped and murdered. She had been left in the cold woods naked and alone. What should we expect from a mom and dad who lived through such an ordeal? Things could never, never be the same.

One person who was a comfort to me was a boy I had been dating during my freshman year of high school. We had become very close before Kathy had been murdered, and he was the one I leaned on when the walls around me seemed to be coming down. Although I didn't really open up to anyone, he was the one person with whom I could share some of what I was going through. I could see in his eyes how he wished there was something he could do to help me. I knew he would do anything to try to ease my pain.

One day I had been crying for some time. Janet and her friend tried to console me and couldn't. Janet asked me if I wanted them to go to the high school and tell him to come to the house, and I said yes. When they got there they approached the principal and asked him if my boyfriend could be released to come and see me. Understandably, he said that he was not authorized to do that.

But Janet and her friend were concerned enough for me that they found him in the building and told him that I needed to talk to him, and he just left. He ran to my house to be with me, to make sure I was okay. Anytime I needed him, he was there for me. One night he was at my house and told me that he had talked to a minister before he got there about what had happened to Kathy. He shared with me what that minister said to him, and it helped, giving me a glimmer of hope that someday things would get better. I was truly thankful he was there for me. It helped. More than I probably let him know.

We began to watch and read some of the news on Kathy's disappearance, about how she was found and about the investigation. As we sat in front of the television watching some of the local news, a friend of my dad's came in. He brought with him a stack of newspapers that he had been collecting about Kathy, thinking that we may want to keep them for the future. I looked at him as my dad took them from his hands and placed them on the sofa. I thought that his gesture was strange. Why would he do that? Why would he think that we would want to sit around and look at her picture, read about how she had been killed and how there were no leads in the case? Janet took the newspapers and put them away, saving them with many other things that were printed. She started a scrapbook of newspaper articles and pictures, memories that she would record for future reference. I didn't look at it; there were things in there I wanted to forget. I couldn't even keep a picture of Kathy out; the memories were too painful.

The questioning became intense after the funeral. Police and detectives were at the house constantly. In any homicide case, they have to question the parents to make sure that they didn't have any involvement in the disappearance or murder of a loved one. My mom and dad were questioned, and it quickly became evident that they had nothing to do with their little girl's death. They asked my dad if he thought Kathy's dog, Tasha, would have tried to protect her if she was attacked. He wasn't sure, so they brought the dog in, and the detective tried approaching my dad in a threatening way. As he did this the dog just lay there with her head down. I didn't think it was unusual. She wasn't my dad's dog. He wasn't the young girl she was attached to.

Tasha had become very depressed since Kathy's death and just moped around the house. That dog was never the same; she knew her master was gone forever. My parents decided to give her to the family across the street, the ones I babysat for after school. The hope was that the young children might love her and pull her out of this depression. I didn't know dogs could get depressed, but this dog was definitely going through some sort of trauma.

We found out later that this family put her down because she tried to bite one of their boys. They told us she never did come around, that her personality stayed the same. It was a sad day when I heard that, and I had wished that my family had been told before it was done. I would have liked to have seen her one more time. I do know that the sadness she displayed was like a human losing a loved one. Had Tasha tried to protect Kathy and couldn't? Did she run all the way home from where she had been left? I know that when she entered the house that night she was in search mode. The anxiety of looking and not finding was unsettling to her; it was evident in her actions.

The detectives went through everything in our room, looking through Kathy's bureau, taking her poems, checking under the bed, searching for something that might give them a clue about where she might have been and whom she was with the night she disappeared. As I watched them manhandle everything, I wanted to tell them to be careful. That's all we had left: her things and our memories. They took the sheets off her bed and noticed a small hole in the mattress. We had bunk beds that were separated, mine on one side of the room and hers on the other. The mattresses were filled with a type of cotton batting, which they proceeded to pull out, ripping the hole larger as they continued. They were feeling around for something that might have been hidden inside. When they finished this task, they left the room, and I just stood there looking at the mess they had made. They didn't bother to put anything back in its place. The stuffing to the mattress just lay on the floor in front of me, and with tears, I bent down and began to put it back. I knew the detectives and police officers had a job to do, but the mentality and method they used was like a bull in a china shop: plowing through, full steam ahead, not caring what precious pieces were broken in the process. Their carelessness would make a lasting negative impact on my life.

During one of the interviews, an officer asked me about a boy my sister Janet dated who had given me a ride home one night. I was near Main Street when he pulled up beside me and asked me if I wanted a ride to my house. I knew who he was, so I didn't hesitate to take the ride. He went to Franklin High School, the same school Janet and I went to, and had also been at our house before, so it wasn't as if he was a stranger. I jumped in, and he headed down the road and made all the turns to take me to my house. As we went up the hill near my home, he passed the first turn to my house. There was another right you could take to get to my house, so I just assumed that he was going to take the next one.

When he passed the second one, I said, "Hey, you missed the turn to my house." As we got to the top of the hill, he looked at me, smiled, and took a right turn.

I said, "Just let me out here. I'll walk the rest of the way home." He had a sinister look on his face, and I knew something wasn't right.

"If you don't stop, I'm going to jump out," I said, and I proceeded to grab for the handle on the door. As I did, he stepped on the gas and continued at a speed that would have caused me great physical harm if I had attempted to jump out of the car.

"Let me out!" I shouted.

His empty eyes looked at me, and he laughed. He went about three miles out, and I began to cry, "Please, just let me go, and I'll walk home." Suddenly he stepped on the brake and began laughing again and told me to get out. I grabbed the handle and got out of the car as fast as I could. He drove down the road a little way, and I saw him take a left turn. Shortly after I started to run, I heard a car and jumped into the bushes on the side of the road to hide. Just barely peeking out, I saw his car approaching. He went by me and continued on. I realized he was coming back to look for me. When he was out of sight, I began to run again. Suddenly I heard the sound of a car, and once again I jumped into the bushes on the side of the road. Slowly his car went by me, and when I couldn't see him anymore, I came out of the bushes and started to run. This continued until I finally got to the top of my hill and my house was in sight. I stood in front of a state trooper's house—he lived two houses from mine—and I finally felt safe. A car came down the hill, and I knew it was him. He stopped in the middle of the road.

He laughed and said, "I was just fooling around. I didn't mean anything by it." He told me to get into the car, and he would bring me home. Did he think I would be that stupid? I could have picked up a rock and almost hit my house from where I was standing.

I yelled at the top of my lungs, "If you don't get out of here, I'm going to wake up the state trooper who lives in this house and tell him what you've done!" After this statement he drove away. I never told my parents or Janet about that night, but I did tell a couple friends.

It was never brought up again until Kathy's death. Some of my friends were interviewed during Kathy's investigation, and they told the police what this guy had done. They asked me about it, and I told them the whole story and how terrified I was. This guy was put on the list of potential suspects and sought out to be questioned.

Another man who was on the list but not brought up in any conversation I had with detectives was a man who used to live upstairs in our home. He and his wife rented from my parents, and I had done a little babysitting for them. Even though there was an incident where this man approached me inappropriately, I did not bring his name up because I didn't relate what had happened to Kathy with what had happened to me in any way. He and his family moved out of our house months before Kathy went missing and was found murdered.

Before he moved out of our house, his wife had asked me to watch their son upstairs while she stepped out to do a few errands. I had no idea that her husband was asleep in the next room. I was tuning in stations on the radio when he came out and sat down beside me. Even then I didn't expect what he was about to do.

He began to touch me inappropriately. I was so scared. Nothing like this had ever happened to me before, and I didn't know what to do. I said "No," as he picked me up and put me on his bed. Just as he put me down, I quickly stood up and ran out the door. He yelled after me, saying, "Karen, just stay and watch the baby. I won't do anything."

I ran across the street to my sister's best friend's house. I was talking to her outside when a car pulled up at the bottom of the hill. He was sitting in the passenger's seat as his wife drove. She yelled for me to come and get my money for babysitting.

I said, "Just keep it." She insisted on giving me the two dollars, so I approached the car. She reached over him and handed the money out the window. He never looked up at me. His eyes were fixed straight ahead, and he wouldn't acknowledge me.

Not long after, they moved out of our house and rented a place somewhere else. I only saw them once after that. My mom, not knowing what had happened to me, told them I would babysit.

I was so angry with her, I said, "Mom, I don't want to sit for them!"

"Karen, I told them you would babysit for them. Just do it this one time."

"Fine," I said. "But don't ever tell someone I'll sit for them again unless you ask me first."

So I reluctantly went to their house and took care of their little boy. He and his wife came home, and he grabbed me and said he would give me a ride home. He pulled me down on his lap, and I said, "No, your wife is giving me a ride." He looked at me with a smile and said, "C'mon, Karen, I'll take you home."

I struggled to get up and repeated, "No, your wife is giving me a ride." Thankfully she stepped forward and said, "I'll take Karen home." I never saw either of them again, not at their home or in town. I assumed that they had moved away, and I was just thankful that I never had to face them again.

The investigation continued. Questions were asked, and people were put on the list of potential suspects. Do you recognize this hat? Do you know whom she might have been with? What was she wearing? Since all the clothes she had on were missing, Ann and Janet went shopping with the police to find replicas of the items. They needed to know what they should be looking for in case they found articles that might belong to her.

We learned that the only things left on her body that cold night were her socks, and that was for a reason. Why leave the socks behind? Knowing the minds of criminals, a criminal profiler would understand that the murderer or someone in his family had serious problems with their feet, maybe to the point of having difficulty walking. Leaving Kathy's socks on might have showed a moment of sympathy for the victim.

It was very difficult to understand the brutality. My thoughts were drawn to questions like: How much did she suffer? What fear did she face, and how much did she struggle to get away? I could see her trying to get away, calling for someone to save her. Did she beg for her life? Did she call out to God to protect her? Or plead with Him to come and save her from the tragedy that was about to take place?

What do people think of when they are about to die? Does their life really flash before their eyes, as I've heard some say? Do they see the ones they love and realize that they will never see them again? Is God with them as death approaches? She was left overnight in the cold on the ground, and even though I know she was dead, it still makes me sad to think she was all alone out there. Why did they have to leave her like that? Did they have no compassion at all? How heartless and cruel a person must be to do such an act. What right do they have to go on and continue their life? Why should they be able to enjoy another day, to take another breath?

CHAPTER NINE

After finding out the details of her murder, I began to look for anything to make me thankful—thankful that she was found right away and not left out in the woods all winter long. There was a big snowstorm the day after she was found, and I was thankful that her body was found right away instead of being found in the spring or never found at all. I was thankful that we were able to bury her in November and didn't have to wait until spring.

I was also thankful for the time I had with her, but I wished it had been more. The cruelty of life was before me, and I was thankful that I still believed in God. Many years after Kathy's death, I was asked how I could possibly believe in God after all life had dished out to me, and I replied, "Because I know He's there. He is the only stable thing in this world of confusion. He never changes. He's always the same."

Regrets were another area that I explored, wishing I had more time with her. Did she know how much I loved her? What if she didn't know that I truly loved her for the person she was? Not just that she was my sister, but that the person she was made a difference in my life. She was gone now, and it was too late to express any of this. Why do we think we have all the time in the world to show people we love them? So many times people think they have tomorrow, and then the tomorrows slip away, and in a moment the one we love is snatched away, taken from us, and our chance to express in words or deeds that their life was important to us is gone.

Death of a loved one is very difficult in itself, but when it is because of unnatural circumstances, the black hole it leaves can never be filled. I missed sharing a future with Kathy; from the day she was taken I began to play out in my head what she would have done with her life. I wondered what her dreams would have been for the future and knew that the future missed out on someone who had much to offer. Her life mattered. It was precious and valuable. Taking her life and the future she would have had was one of the most evil acts that a person could have done.

Thanksgiving was approaching, and none of us cared. To tell you the truth, I didn't remember it was Thanksgiving until people began to bring food over to the house. They brought turkey with all the fixings and extra food to carry us through weeks to come. My appetite was at zero. The thought of food brought on nausea, and nothing was appealing. None of us had a desire to eat much of anything. I worried about my mom because she was already so thin. She definitely couldn't afford to lose any weight, so we encouraged her to eat. Thanksgiving Day was extremely difficult; we hardly acknowledge it. Christmas was around the corner, and I hated that we would not have Kathy with us.

How painful it would be to know that the holiday would come and go without her. It would be another mountain to climb and another twist of the knife in our hearts.

How do you celebrate when your life has been torn and your heart weeps? We didn't. I just prayed that Thanksgiving Day would go by as quickly as possible so it would be in the past and not the present. I would do the same when Christmas Day arrived.

In the future, I felt pain for anyone who lost a loved one during the holidays. My heart went out to them and the sorrow they experienced during a time that should be full of happiness, spent with family and friends. Every Thanksgiving and Christmas they will be reminded of their loss, as I am. In time I learned to cling to the loved ones I still had and make memories with them that would last a lifetime. Would I forget the past? Never, but I thanked God for the ones that He'd left behind. I'd cherish the time with them, look to the future, and deal with the past as best I could.

Sisters are different flowers
from the same garden.

UNKNOW
*

CHAPTER TEN

As the investigation continued, we tried to press on. I questioned how we could continue, and the words "one day at a time" played over and over in my head. I relived the past every day, and every day was a struggle. I couldn't think ahead. I couldn't see any hope in the future. I could only think about getting through the current day. When tomorrow came, then I'd think about getting through that day. I couldn't look to the future. It was much too difficult.

I lived in the present and also in the past; that's just the way it was. If this was so difficult for me, I couldn't even imagine how awful it was for my parents. It hurt to think about them and the pain they were going through.

All of this took so much energy; just opening my eyes in the morning, knowing the day had begun, brought on a feeling of exhaustion. Every one of us was tired. It took great effort to perform any daily task. I had to go back to school soon, but I had no desire to move forward.

I knew in my heart that there was a God; I never doubted that as a child. I believed God could be everywhere, see and hear everything, and was in control of what could or could not happen. So even without knowing Christ as my Saviour or having an understanding of how He could allow Kathy to be murdered, I called out to Him in that time of sorrow. I took a deep breath and asked God to give me strength for the day. There were times I wondered if He knew just how much pain I was feeling. Did He understand how awful it was for my family? "Mom is angry with you, God, very angry. Help her to understand it's not You who has brought on such evil. You would never be part of something so wicked."

Janet and I had a tough road ahead of us. Our parents' road would be tougher. I felt them drifting away. To lose a sister this way was horrible, but to lose your child in such a brutal way was unbearable. The future didn't exist for them, and the task of raising two daughters still at home was something they couldn't grasp. They didn't have the energy for it. The past was sucking the life right out of them. Within the walls of our home, the loneliness would intensify—four people living together but having a very hard time communicating, each carrying a great burden, overwhelming pain, and yes, guilt. Feelings of guilt because none of us could change a thing about what had happened to Kathy. Our minds were tormented with thoughts of what ifs. We were headed down different roads, and we couldn't find a connecting path.

Rumors began to fly; the suspect list began to grow. How could there be so many men in this little town who might have committed such a crime? Growing up here, I never would have suspected it, never would have thought our tiny town had such evil in it. Somebody must know something. It's not as though things go on in a place like this and word doesn't get around. One man was on the top of the list as a suspect, and much of the focus and attention seemed to be on him.

One night shortly after Kathy's death, my dad left the house in a distraught state of mind. He left with a shotgun and met up with others to search for the person or persons who might have been involved. As a dad, he was tormented by the knowledge of what had happened to his little girl. I know my dad would have done anything to protect her if he could have. He definitely would have hurt someone that night if he had known for sure who killed Kathy and where they were. Thankfully he came home that night not having done harm to anyone. I watched him come through the door with such stress visible on his face. He had been crying and had such an expression of emptiness. When he sat down, I went over to talk to him and said, "Dad, how do you know for sure your vengeance would be taken out on the right person? If you hurt the wrong man, it accomplishes nothing. You need to let the police handle this." He just looked at me and cried. I hugged him until he got up and walked away. How does a father handle such agony? It is his job, his responsibility, to protect his beloved children. How does he face the brutal truth that he was unable to protect her? My dad never did. Even though he knew in his head that under the circumstances there wasn't anything he could have done, my dad's heart told him otherwise. His heart continued to beat the words, "Why wasn't I there to protect her?"

I reviewed the stages of events over and over, looking for anything I could have done to change the outcome. There must have been something I could have done to stop this from happening. I often wished it had been me instead of her. I felt guilty just for being alive when she wasn't. But my guilt would never change the fact that she was gone.

CHAPTER ELEVEN

After Ann, Roger, and Richard went back to their homes, the task of dealing with the police fell on Janet and me. They continued to ask questions in hopes that we could shed some light on what happened that dreadful night. No matter how hard we thought and tried to remember something that might lead the detectives in the right direction, we couldn't. I would say to myself, "Just think, Karen. There must be something you can remember that might make a difference." I replayed the events as they happened over and over in my mind, but nothing new was revealed. Then I'd cry as the feeling of helplessness came crashing down.

As the police became more frustrated, they were careless in the way they treated my family. They accused Janet of hiding something or protecting someone. "Who is it? Tell us who it is?"

Janet stood there, looked them in the eyes, and with tears blurted out, "If I knew who did this to her and I had a gun, don't you think I would use it?"

She was crushed by the accusation. Before Roger left for Germany an officer said, "For all we know, it could have been you."

He replied, "Well, that would be pretty difficult, since I just flew in from Germany, where I was serving my country."

Many worked very hard on the case and wanted to see it solved, but the frustration and inexperience of others brought about stupidity in some of the questioning. Mistakes were made; some were made because there was a lack of expertise in knowing how to ask the right questions in a homicide case. They worked with what they had, using regular police officers instead of detectives to do interviews, dressing them up in suits and sending them out to fill the void of detectives. They were not trained for homicide cases, and it was inevitable that there would be mistakes made.

A homicide in Franklin did not happen very often. The small town was not prepared to take on the task, and it would show in some of the details of the case. At first we did not question them or doubt that everything was being done to solve the case and to bring in those who were a part of this horrendous crime. However, as time passed, we began to question their motives. Doubting the police made things more difficult for my family.

With all that was going on, we found it hard to go back to anything normal. None of us were even sure what normal was anymore. We had been so consumed with the investigation that the thought of stepping outside of that was a little terrifying. For me, the thought of going back to school made me nauseated. I didn't want to leave home. My mom walked up to me one day and said, "Karen, you have to go

back to school. I know it's going to be hard, but you've got to go back."
I sat there and cried.

Going back to school was one of the most difficult things I had to do. I was a high school sophomore, and it should have been a time to anticipate, but I was dreading it. I wanted to know how I was supposed to go back to normal activities. How would people treat me? Would my friends be there for me? Since this had happened, I had not talked to anyone about what I was going through. How do you explain to a friend that you wished you had died instead of your sister? How can anyone understand how it feels to have no relief from your pain?

I walked into the doors of my high school and immediately felt that I didn't belong anymore. I felt as though I was outside looking in, as if I was watching a movie. I saw what was going on, but I couldn't seem to jump in and be a part of it. Very few people approached me. No one knew what to say to me, and I didn't know what to say to them. So we said nothing. Silence is not the best way to deal with a crisis in your life.

I didn't share my feelings at home or with my friends at school. It was as if mentioning it was forbidden, and I began to keep what I was feeling inside. I walked off alone to cry and made a promise to myself: I wasn't going to show anyone how badly it hurt, and I wasn't going to cry in front of them. Inside, I was barely hanging on.

My friends went on with their lives. They had their studies, sports, and cheerleading. Practice as usual, hanging out with friends, and laughing in the hallways. All the things I thought were important suddenly didn't seem so important at all. I felt so disconnected. I had been involved in cheerleading since seventh grade, and it was something I always felt very excited about. I had looked forward to continuing it in high school, but now none of that seemed to matter.

Knowing what happened to Kathy made me feel as if I had no right to enjoy life again. What right did I have to be happy or to participate in and enjoy any school events? My sister had been murdered, taken away from her family in one of the most brutal ways one could think of. I had no right to be happy, to laugh, or to think that someday the heartache I was experiencing would ever get better.

The rest of the school year lingered on but finally ended. I usually loved summer. Summer meant days in the sun and time spent on the beach hanging out with friends. This summer all I wanted was to be left alone. I was tired of faking that I was okay. I had things to figure out, and I couldn't do it with all these people around me.

In the fall of 1972, I became a sophomore and Kathy would have been entering her freshman year. I was never going to experience what it was like to have my younger sister in high school with me. Being one grade apart, I'm sure we would have attended a lot of events together. I wasn't going to see her participate in high school activities or find out what her interests would have been.

Would she have played sports? She was athletic. I thought she would have been great on the high school track team. She certainly was built to be a runner. Would she have excelled academically? Would she have hung out with me at football and basketball games? What would she have pursued after graduation? We would never share our dreams for the future.

Every event throughout the rest of the year was a battle to get through. Her birthday came and went without acknowledgement—no songs of happy birthday and no cake.

There were so many things I was going to miss out on by not having my kid sister around. Laughing until you drop to the floor because you can't breathe anymore. Crying and holding each other when one was in pain, knowing the other felt it too. All of this was taken away because someone else saw no value in a young girl's life.

People continued to withdraw from me because they didn't know what they should or shouldn't say. I withdrew from them because it was easier than trying to act normal. No one in my family received any counseling. In 1971, free counseling after a tragedy wasn't available like it is today. My family didn't have the money to pay for counseling for me or Janet. My mom was seeing someone to help her cope, but back then the emphasis on a child needing counseling was not as important as it is today.

Today, counselors are immediately at schools when a classmate is murdered or killed in a car accident, but I had no one to help me open up about the trauma of having a sister murdered. I would have to learn to deal with all that was thrown at me in spite of the pain and emptiness I felt. Life went on whether I wanted it to or not.

At times, I thought about what I could do to stop the stabbing pain in my heart. Taking my own life came to mind, but I knew I couldn't do that to my parents. They had gone through enough. They would not be able to survive losing another child, especially that way. I came to that realization after I expressed to a friend that I wanted to end my life. She looked at me angrily and said, "Go ahead." Her words sent me over the edge.

I went home and took quite a few aspirins, which made me very sick. As I began to throw up, my dad stood over me and said, "What is wrong with you?" I looked at him with tears in my eyes and said, "I'm just not feeling well." That's when I realized how selfish it would be to take my own life. How could I do that to them?

I needed someone to come along and show me how to get through all of this, but there was no one I could talk to. It would have made a difference if someone could have just told me that what I was feeling was normal and that I wasn't alone. Nothing could make the pain go away, but at least it would have given me a way to deal with the steps of grieving. After that foolish attempt to end my life, I decided that I would not lie down and die today or any other day. I looked up and spoke softly, "Please, God, help me find my way."

CHAPTER TWELVE

Time moved on, but I seemed to stand still in the past. I tried desperately to take one step at a time. "Just one baby step at a time," I told myself. The ongoing investigation was a constant reminder of what happened. I wasn't able to let go but did progress as many months went by, thinking that any step forward was hope for the future. Some days I would take a step back and lose a little bit of what I was holding on to. The next day I would try again, and some light would shine through, illuminating the way to hope.

I laughed one day, and the guilt was tremendous. What right did I have? How could I? Kathy was gone, and no one had been arrested. It had been months since her death, but still I scolded myself. "How dare you, Karen? How could you laugh or feel any happiness? How can you enjoy life knowing what happened to her?" The voice in my head rebuked me until I felt I should be punished for my laughter. What if someone thought I didn't care anymore, or that Kathy wasn't in my daily thoughts? If others heard me laugh, they might think everything was okay, and they'd start to forget her. I might start to forget her. It was already hard to remember certain things about her. I tried to hold on to the memories I had—how she walked, the way she talked, her smile, and her laugh. Where did they go? I felt them slowly slipping away.

Eventually I did laugh again, and although I felt guilty each time I laughed, I began to realize that it was okay. I began to understand that laugher didn't diminish the love I had for her or the empty space left in my life, nor did it hinder my desire to see whoever was involved brought to justice. Each time I smiled or laughed, I would whisper to myself, "It's okay, Karen. You can be happy again. It doesn't change the fact that you love her and miss her."

The police continued to ask questions about the events leading up to Kathy's disappearance and murder. They always came back, wondering if we could remember anything else that would help them—something she said, someone she knew, places she'd been that would give them some direction. Did she have a diary or journal where she might have written things down that she didn't want anyone else to read? It always made me feel as though I was missing something. Why couldn't I remember anything that might help them find out what happened to her? My mind was constantly searching for answers. No matter how hard I tried, nothing was revealed.

From time to time, I would remember some little thing that I wasn't sure would make a difference, but I would tell the police anyway, hoping that they might connect it with what they already knew. Not being there to help her when she needed it most compelled me to help find those involved. I had to help in some way. The desire to see justice served grew strong in me. They had to pay for what they had done to her. Justice was all that mattered—justice for Kathy, and for the family and friends she left behind.

The night Kathy was murdered, we not only lost Kathy; we lost our security. We lost our innocence. Kathy's life had great value, and it was cruelly and unjustly taken. Would we ever see justice?

I hoped justice would help soothe the guilt. I felt guilty because I didn't know most of the answers the detectives asked me: Who were her friends? Where did she go? Did she share any secrets with me? I realized I had been so self-involved. As a freshman in high school, I let friends and school activities take over my life, my thoughts, my time.

Kathy had been in eighth grade, and I had moved on to high school. In just a few months I was living in a different world. I had left her behind, and in those short few months before her death, I lost the connection we had. High school was so different from junior high, and I was busy exploring my new world. In the process, I lost touch with what was going on in hers.

What had she been up to? Where had she been going? Who was she hanging around with? All these questions would be asked of me after she died, and it saddened me to not have the answers to any of them. Were there things she didn't share with me? No one in my family really shared much with one another. We lived day-to-day, doing what needed to be done, going where we needed to go, and not bothering one another with the details.

Kathy was rather quiet and introverted. She expressed herself through her poetry, which she didn't share with many. As I read her poetry, it revealed a sadness I didn't know she had. How could I have not known that this was how she felt about certain things? I was so angry with myself for not knowing her better, and now it was too late.

I lived with more than just guilt. I lived with fear. I was afraid of things I had never been afraid of before. I was afraid of each day and of the future. I was afraid of losing another sibling. Would something terrible happen to Janet as well? I wondered if the people involved were watching my house or watching me. Would they come after me? My imagination trapped me inside a menacing world. Fear caused my heart to race. Any joy or peace I had in life was turned upside down in a pile of rubble. How could I calm the fears that shadowed me during the day and suffocated me in the darkness of night?

Nothing would ever be the same. I couldn't walk anywhere without being afraid. I was afraid to take a shower unless somebody was in the house with me. When I showered, I never closed my eyes; and I did it as fast as I could. I didn't want to be alone in the house at all. Sometimes at night I would hear things, and my imagination would start to whirl. Any unfamiliar noise kept me awake and made me wonder if someone was there. I positioned myself as if I was on guard until I finally fell asleep from exhaustion. Morning would come, and I'd get up and go to school, trying to function with the little sleep I had the night before. I still had to walk to school, but now I listened for footsteps behind me or a car slowly pulling up beside me. Being on alert every waking hour was exhausting.

CHAPTER THIRTEEN

More than a year had gone by, and our time at the police station grew less. As the police got deeper into the investigation, we began to feel disconnected from them. We didn't have a constant flow of police and investigators in and out of our home anymore. Our detachment from the everyday involvement of the case brought on new emotions. What's happening? Have they found anything new? Are they working on it daily? Do they still care? Is the investigation going strong, or are they pulling back? As detectives began to work on other crimes, I began to wonder if the intensity for Kathy's case was less. I asked God to never let them forget, and to never let them feel hopeless in solving her murder. "Please, God, don't let them ever forget her."

I wished we had an advocate to plead for us, and keep us updated on what was going on. My parents couldn't do it; they barely could get through the day. If they were in constant contact with the police, it would surely kill them. Getting through the day consumed them. I was fifteen, and I kept thinking I should know more of what I should do.

I wasn't even sure if I could call the police and inquire about what was going on. I would like to say that the men and women working on the investigation were all well trained for a homicide case, but that wasn't true. First of all, I never talked to a woman who worked on the initial investigation. The men asked questions that were very personal and uncomfortable to answer. Some of the subject matter was embarrassing to talk about as a fifteen-year-old.

Also, not all were trained in the field of investigation or had worked in the major crimes unit. Some didn't know what to look for, the questions to ask. They didn't know how to recognize if a piece of the puzzle was fitting or not fitting, or to pay attention to the smallest of details and to make a connection no matter how tiny it may be. Were there people on the case who were trained, qualified to do this job? Yes. Were there people who gave their all trying to solve it? Yes. But I couldn't help feeling that something was missing, that there had to be more that they could do to solve this crime.

I knew in my heart that someone had information that could help solve this brutal murder. Someone was out there who wasn't the killer but knew the details of what had happened to her, and they wouldn't come forward.

As days turned into months and months turned into years, the connection we had to the investigation dwindled. We didn't know if they had found out anything new or if there were any new leads. Had there been other suspects added to the original list? Once, they had asked me about my uncle. They wanted to know if he had ever done anything inappropriate to me. I told them no, he had never done anything. But this made me wonder how many were actually on the list. When we did inquire about the investigation, they just told us that they were still working hard on it but supplied no answers.

After a while we began to lose hope that they would ever arrest those involved. We realized they couldn't reveal evidence or whom they had talked to, but nothing made us feel they were making progress. I tried to believe that justice would be done. I said to myself, "They'll figure it out; we just need to be patient." There had to be a trail left behind, one that led to her disappearance and murder. In this small town someone had to know something.

In a place this small, people knew the affairs of other families. Gossip spread quickly. Someone had a key to open the door to all the mysteries that lay in the past. For the longest time I lived with the feeling that at any moment an arrest would be made; justice would be served. That finally I'd be able to say to my sister, "There, Kathy, they got him. He'll pay for what he did, and he won't be able to hurt anyone else." But as time went by, that hope began to fade like the evening sun falling swiftly behind the mountains.

The hope of seeing my parents grow closer together through this horrific ordeal began to vanish also. Deep into their grief they fell, but not into the arms of each other; they fell deeper into whatever would give them relief from the pain. Alcohol and prescription drugs took a toll on them. They reached out, like so many others, for whatever would give them relief from the pain. I didn't blame them; maybe if I was older at the time I would have done the same thing. I watched them and knew that those things didn't give them the results they wanted. They wanted the hurt to stop, and every day they woke up and it was still there, staring them right in the face.

I wanted them to cling to each other for comfort and find some joy in knowing they had children still at home who loved them no matter what. But they found comfort in no one— not us and not with each other. The memories of Kathy were too painful for them, of her as their baby, their little girl, and of the life so brutally snatched away. Their tormented minds would not heal or find a place of relief; not now and, I feared, not in years to come.

CHAPTER FOURTEEN

Staying in our house became a tremendous strain on my mom and dad, and they decided to sell. Everywhere I turned I saw memories. She slept here, walked there, and made us laugh when ...

Staying in the room we shared was difficult, and was a constant reminder that I had a baby sister who was now gone. In my mind I would imagine her walking around in the room, sleeping in her bed, thinking about the conversation we would have in the morning. Though it was hard to feel the presence of her there, it was more difficult to leave that house and the connection I had with her because of it. It was the only place where I could hold on to the reality of her life, to close my eyes and remember the smell of her, the sound of her voice, and her tomboy look. I didn't want to let that go.

The house went on the market, and within a short amount of time it sold. It was bought by someone who wanted to help the family in their own way, and had plans to make it a rental property. The day we packed our things to move into an apartment not far away was a very sad day for me. With tears, I reluctantly put my belongings into boxes. It reminded me of the day that Kathy's things were removed from the room we shared. I stood in my room, closed my eyes, and tried to commit it all to memory. "Please don't let me forget this time and this place I shared with her."

Somehow it felt like I was abandoning her. I was leaving the one place that gave me a connection to her, the common ground we had together, her life and mine. It was our room, the place we did back-bends and played marbles on the floor. Where we talked at night and got dressed for school in the morning. It was where she wrote poetry and I practiced my cheerleading. When we were punished, this was the room we were sent to.

It was here she swore up and down that she heard Santa Claus outside the window by her bed Christmas Eve. I knew it had been my dad with bells in hand jingling away and shouting "Ho, ho, ho," but I didn't have the heart to tell her. She so believed in Santa Claus at the time and was very confident that it was him visiting us that night. It was in this room, by that window, I saw her walk by in my dream.

The dream was so real that for days when I went to bed at night I would look for her outside my window. As my family was getting ready to leave, I stood in my room—our room—and whispered, "I don't want to go, Kathy. I'm sorry. I want to stay here with you, to cling to the things that remind me of your life. I don't want to let go of your presence here, of the imagination I've created in this room so I can cope. The one where I pretend that you're on a trip and soon you'll be home and life will be as it once was."

The car moved slowly out of the driveway, and I couldn't help feeling that I was really saying goodbye to her. I understood why my parents didn't want to live there; the constant reminder of Kathy was too much for them. But the thought of someone else living in our house, sleeping in the bedroom I shared with her, was disturbing. I continued to keep my eyes focused on the house until it wasn't in view anymore. I watched the windows to our bedroom disappear, and under my breath I said, "Goodbye."

As we approached the apartment and went in, it was unfamiliar territory. It was a place that didn't have the constant reminders of her existence. My bedroom didn't have her bed or bureau in it. This room did not give me the feeling of her presence nearby. I closed my eyes in this new bedroom and could not imagine her walking from her bed to her bureau. Her place wasn't at the table when we ate, and she wasn't standing next to me as I washed and she dried the dishes. In our old house, I could close my eyes, and a certain smell would conjure up a memory of her. I knew that she had existed there, that she had been real. I'd lose all that; I knew I would.

As I unpacked my things, I decided not to keep a photo of Kathy out in my room. Though I knew what had happened to her was true, I began to find a way to cope with the emptiness of not having her there. I trained myself to immediately think of something else when thoughts of her started to take over. Sometimes I would sing and then make lists of what I needed to do or where I would like to go someday.

I occupied my mind with anything so I wouldn't fall into the steps of reliving her murder. That's the reason I didn't place a picture of her in my room, because seeing her would instantly bring me to that place. There were so many other things to remember about her, but the fact that she was raped and murdered seemed to consume anything else. I realized that whoever did this not only instilled guilt and fear in me but also was robbing me of the beautiful memories I had of her.

The first night in the apartment, I cried for a long time. I hated being there. This was not my home. Why did everything have to be so different? I longed for the days before Kathy died, and I didn't want to leave our childhood memories behind. I wanted to remember how Ann used to hold Kathy and call her Monkey because she would wrap her legs around Ann's waist so tightly. I wanted to go back to the days of jump rope, marbles, and kick the can. Those are the stories I wanted to recall—not the horrible way she died. How do I get there? How do I bypass the gruesome to get to the beautiful? I didn't know how.

What about the people working on her case? Had they forgotten how important it was to find those involved and make sure that they paid for the disgusting crime they had committed? Was she important to them anymore? Would there ever be closure for my family?

Years slipped away, and so did the urgency to solve her murder. No longer was there an expectation that the killer would be found. The hope that those who committed this crime would be caught had slipped away. I still wanted the police to treat the case as a priority, but it was evident that it wasn't. I knew they had other cases to work on, but I didn't want them to stop trying to solve Kathy's murder. Why couldn't it be a priority now? Not only in 1971, but in any other year that would pass by. There would never be closure until those involved were caught and had paid for the despicable thing they had done.

CHAPTER FIFTEEN

There came a day when I didn't think about Kathy, and it made me cry. The following day a thought of her came to me, and it was then I realized that the previous day had gone by without one thought of her. Since the time of her death, there had not been one day I didn't have some thought concerning her. I had been able to suppress some of my thoughts so she didn't consume my day. I had never gone a whole day without thinking about her at least once.

I was shocked with the knowledge that I had gone an entire day and didn't have one small thought of her in my mind. I sat down and put my hands to my face and sobbed. How could I have gone through a whole day without thinking about her at least once? Was it a sign that I was beginning to forget her? For some time I purposely did things to make sure that another day wouldn't go by without remembering her. It was an exhausting way to live.

The investigation went on all through my high school years, but we rarely ever heard from the police or the detectives anymore.

Because of that, there wasn't a constant reminder of November 21, 1971, the day she was found murdered. Even though her murder wasn't discussed as frequently, she certainly wasn't forgotten by anyone in my family.

I didn't enjoy my high school years. Mostly I just wanted to graduate and get out of there. I tried to fit in, and it may have looked like I did; but I didn't. I portrayed the illusion that I was having fun, but deep within me a battle raged. There was a constant battle to feel normal and to try to forget the awful thing that had been done to my sister and the path of destruction it left behind. Over the years there would be times that I would pretend as long as I could that I was the youngest, and the sister with whom I had shared a room with didn't exist. It's not that I wanted to forget her, but it was just easier for me to cope with the fact that she was gone. By doing this, I could go longer periods of time without the awful remembrance of the crime that was committed.

Then one day a memory would be triggered by something I saw or smelled in the air, and just like that I would be thrown back into the ocean of memories, swimming against the waves of depression and gasping for air. Sometimes it would take days to get over this feeling, and then I would play the game again so I could escape from the constant beating those memories gave me. Off and on throughout my high school years I would play the game to help me function in everyday life. I never knew how long it would be before memories of that day would creep back in—recalling the night she went missing, searching for her, finding out she was brutally raped and murdered.

The picture of my family sitting in the living room in tears as the doctor gave my mom a shot to make her sleep, police present, is one that is embedded deep.

At times my way of pretending she never lived, caused me to feel guilty, but it enabled me to go longer periods of time when the pain would not be so intense. Sometimes when a detective would contact my family I would say to myself, "Why are they here, and who are they talking about? Why would we know about that? They must have the wrong family." Of course, deep down I knew that it was my little sister, Kathy, they were talking about. I was never able to totally escape to a place of denial, just to a place of coping the best way I knew how.

Shortly after my senior graduation, I married Mike, my high school sweetheart. We had children right away, and Mike and the girls occupied my time. There were days when I struggled with Kathy's death, but it became easier. Even after eight years, I still had times where something would trigger a memory, and I'd drift back to that place I fought to forget. But at least now I was able to dwell on some of the sweet memories of her and not only on the ugliness of her death. I concentrated on my family, and because of the experiences I went through, I tried to make sure that they knew I had a great love for them. We have all heard the motto, "Never go to bed angry with someone." I tried to live by that motto. I didn't always succeed, but it was important for me to try.

The family I had now kept me focused and satisfied. They gave me purpose and goals in my life. I wanted to be a good wife to my husband, and a good mother to my children. Being a young couple with children was not easy. We struggled the first five years of our marriage as we learned to grow as a couple and to adapt to the role of mom and dad. Mike and my daughters, Joscelyn and Melissa, were bundles of hope for me. I still wanted whoever killed Kathy to be caught and justice served, but I no longer lived my days in the past.

Mike worked hard to provide for our family, and I worked hard taking care of Mike, the girls, and our home. It wasn't easy, downright difficult at times, but I had lived a life of "not easy" for so long that I was ready for rough roads ahead. Sometimes I would get battered and bruised along the way, but a healing eventually came. It was the enduring part that could be wearisome—to not give up during the storm so that I would be around to see the peace approach. That was truly the most difficult part—not giving up.

CHAPTER SIXTEEN

Even though my family's religious background was Catholic, I had never seen my brother Richard care about spiritual things. But one day he came home, and I saw a change in him. He talked to my mom about claiming Christ as his own, and she wasn't happy about it. He was a caring and loving person before God seemed important in his life, but now it was different. There wasn't an emphasis on him and what he wanted to achieve. It was on God and how could he serve Him. He went on to seminary school, became a minister, and had a beautiful wife and son.

So many times in life, on top of what a person has already endured comes another test of durability. The day I got the phone call that Richard had passed away was one of those days. As a little boy, Richard had open-heart surgery to replace a valve that wasn't functioning properly, and all these years he had been fine. But then the doctors discovered bleeding around his heart, and he went in for another surgery. He had an aneurism so large that they couldn't believe it hadn't burst. They took care of the aneurysm, but his condition continued to worsen.

I couldn't believe there would be another funeral for a sibling who had died way before their time. It didn't seem possible that my parents would lay to rest another child. Richard's heart was weak because of a valve that wasn't functioning properly, but to me, his heart wasn't weak or small; it was bigger than most in the way he loved.

My fondest memory of him was the day of Kathy's funeral. I remember crying and feeling an arm come around my shoulders; it was Richard. His eyes told me he loved me and wished he could make it all go away. Richard and his wife were good people; they were godly and had a beautiful son. How would his wife and son manage without him? How would my parents deal with the loss of another child? How would we as siblings deal with yet another loss, this time of a brother? How was I going to make sense of any of this? This was not supposed to happen.

We prepared to travel to Pennsylvania for Richard's funeral. We rented a bigger car, and my dad, Janet and her boyfriend, my husband, Mike, and I rode together to attend yet another day of saying goodbye to someone we loved. My mom made a decision to not go; she was devastated and couldn't face saying goodbye to another one of her children.

She had been through this before, and somehow not seeing him helped her deal with his death. To cope with the loss of Kathy, I pretended I didn't have a younger sister. Maybe this was her way of pretending, making up her own story so she could cope. Sometimes when the pain is as deep as it can go, you do whatever it takes to survive, and Mom was definitely in that place.

Dad looked empty. I didn't know how to comfort him. The look in his eyes was a look I'd seen before; it had become a familiar one since Kathy's death. His expression of hopelessness was one of the saddest ones I'd ever encountered. I saw life spring up in him when Joscelyn and Melissa were around him. They had a way of bringing a glow, a sparkle, back into his life that usually wasn't there. Children can take us to places we can't seem to get to on our own.

After seeing another one of his children placed into the ground, I prayed that he would hold on to the joy he received from grandchildren who gave him unconditional love. They gave him all the kisses and hugs he could ask for, not based upon his performance as a pepé or hindered by the memories of the past. It's a magic that children possess and is often overlooked.

At the funeral home, we stood in line waiting to see Richard's wife and son. As with Kathy's funeral, there were a lot of people who attended, and it portrayed a man who was loved by many. I could hear the same voice telling me not go in as I did when Kathy died. I turned around to walk away and said, "I can't go in there. I can't."

Janet stood behind me and with her hand nudged me to move forward. "You can do this; be strong," she whispered.

I walked slowly through the line, and I began to make a list of regrets in my mind. The regrets list—I had made one at Kathy's funeral and now was making one for Richard. I wished I had gone to the hospital to see him before he died; the last time Richard and I were together was for his wedding years before. I wished I had known him and his family better.

I wished we had at least stayed in contact with each other by phone or letter, but we didn't. It seemed that no one in my family stayed in touch with each other unless they lived in New Hampshire. I didn't want my family to be strangers to one another.

I thought that when my girls are grown up and have children, I want it to be different. I want to stay close to them and to any grandchildren I might have. I wanted to be part of their lives through the triumphs, joys and especially through the times of defeat and sorrow. As I pondered my regrets, I wondered if there would always be regrets when a loved one died, wishing you had done things differently and realizing that when it's too late. With life far from being perfect, there would always be some regrets, but it was important to try to make them as few as possible.

I approached Richard's wife and gave her a hug, expressing how bad I felt that she had lost her husband, and that their son, who was only three years old, had lost his dad. She in return expressed her sadness that I had lost a brother. With sympathetic eyes, she looked at me and said, "I just want to warn you that Richard looks different from when you saw him last. He lost a lot of weight in the hospital."

As soon as she said that, my throat started to tighten and close up. I said, "I'm sorry my mom couldn't be here, but she just couldn't bring herself to come." With a nod from her, I headed to where my brother lay in the casket to say goodbye and tell him I loved him.

How much better it would have been to tell him how much I loved him while he was alive, not after he had passed from this life to eternity. As I approached the casket, I could feel myself shaking. I knelt down in front of him, and memories of him flooded my mind; some brought a smile and some sadness. I remembered him as funny but mostly serious. He always seemed to know the direction he wanted to take in life.

He excelled academically, was in the exchange student program, and finished a course through the Outward Bound program. I remember how badly he wanted to go to Outward Bound, and the possibility of doing it was slim because of his heart condition. Through physicals and a doctor's approval he was able to go, and was determined that even though he had a heart condition, he was going to finish the course. That was Richard; he had tenacity to accomplish the task that was set before him.

Mostly I remembered him as kind and caring, except for the time he said, "Hey, look. I can pick you up by your neck," and proceeded to do so. He thought it was a cool trick, until I started to choke, and then in a panic he put me down. His look of surprise told me that his thought process was far from being intelligent. He repeatedly told me he was sorry.

Another memory that flashed before my eyes was of his concern for me just before his wedding. I had some stomach issues and was in pain. Richard talked to me for a while, and I explained to him that I had had this problem before. He wanted to make sure that Mom had taken me to the doctor. He was so sweet and tender.

An older sister is a friend and defender –
a listener, conspirator, a counselor and
a sharer of delights. And sorrows too.

PAM BROWN

CHAPTER SEVENTEEN

After Richard died, I once again questioned why any of us existed and what our purpose was here on earth. There had to be more to life than just existing. I knew in my heart, as Richard did, that it had something to do with God. I desperately needed to understand exactly what it was.

After returning home from the funeral, I felt something missing in my life. I had the girls and Mike, and I valued that; but the direction my life was taking was not good. I had a definite hole that needed to be filled. When the road I was on revealed to me a huge sign that said, "Dead end; turn around," God spoke softly and said, "Just come with Me, and I'll show you the way."

I had many conversations with God over the years, about Kathy and then about Richard. I questioned why He didn't step in and stop what happened. Even though I knew God would never have a part in evil, I felt that maybe, just maybe, He ought to take a little more control of things here on earth.

"I know we have free will and all, but don't You think it's time to at least step in and protect the children of this world? So what do you think, God? Maybe just protect the children; is that so much to ask?"

I had this conversation with Him a number of times, and the outcome never seemed to change. I continued to try to figure it all out—life, the purpose for life. Why do some people suffer through life more than others? What's beyond the here and now? Was there really eternity?

I prayed, "God, please give me some answers. I'm walking a very thin line. There has to be hope in something more than just ourselves. I want to be a good mom to the girls, and I want more for Mike and our family. I know you are a key to our happiness, but I can't seem to find exactly what I'm looking for. If you could just show me what I am supposed to do, I would be thankful."

I knew people who had it all but were miserable, and I knew people who had nothing, and their lives were empty also. I had come to the conclusion that whether you were rich or poor, your life could still be empty. This revealed to me that material things couldn't fulfill one's life. It had to be something else, and I decided to see if it was church.

The following Sunday I went to church alone. I listened to the priest speak, and I walked out feeling exactly the same as when I walked in. I decided that it was just because I needed to go more than once, so the following Sunday I headed off to church. Once again I left feeling the same as when I walked in.

Well, I thought, I believe that to find purpose in life and answers to my questions definitely involves God, but this is not the way to find it. What I'm looking for is not here; it's not in a church building or in church itself. God, I'm asking You to help me find the way. I know You are all-powerful and know all things. You see all things, and You are everywhere. Please, God, I know You are busy, and I am just one person, but if You could find the time to show me the way I would really appreciate it.

Shortly after that conversation with God, Mike and the girls and I were invited to a Christmas program at a church close to our home. Joscelyn was in a small private kindergarten that was run by two women who went to this small church. Little did I know that both of these women had been praying for me and my family for months.

We attended the Sunday school Christmas program, and later in the week two men showed up at our front door, Bibles in hand. They wanted to speak with Mike and me about the Bible. We turned them away because at that moment we were having a going-away party for my husband's brother, who had joined the service and was leaving to serve his country.

Another week passed by, and two different men were facing me at my front door. They too carried Bibles and wanted to speak with us about God's Word. I thought what is up with these people? Are they going to show up every week now?

I explained to them that my husband wasn't home, and they asked if it was possible to come back the next week when Mike would be home so they could talk with both of us. They were so polite and kind.

I thought, why not? We agreed on a day for them to revisit us and then said goodbye.

Mike came home that night, and I informed him of the visit from the two men and how they were going to come back the following week to show us some things in the Bible. "Why didn't you tell them we weren't interested?"

"They were so polite and nice, I didn't want to tell them no."

My character trait of not saying no got us into trouble more than once. Well, the discussion Mike and I had after that was definitely headed in the direction of not wanting them to come back, but there was nothing I could do. I didn't have their names or phone numbers, so they were going to show up whether we wanted them to or not.

B day came, B for Bible, and the two men were expected to visit us that night. You would think that I would anticipate this. After all, I was searching for truth, purpose, and direction in my life, looking for answers to all those questions. Going back to church had brought me to the conclusion that whatever truth I needed wasn't in a building, in material things, or in a person. My gut told me it was with God, but I was still searching for what that was. So why was I regretting that I had told these men they could come back? They just wanted to show us some things in the Bible. What harm could that do? We could use a little religion in our lives, as things aren't going so well.

All day long I thought about the response I was going to give them when they asked me a question. If they say this, I'll say that. I continued this self-question-and-answer game throughout the day.

Mike came home and told me that while he was at work he kept thinking about the men who were going to come and talk to us. I laughed and told him that I had been the same way all day. He said, "Is there any reason why you couldn't have just told them no? That we weren't interested and not to bother coming back?"

Again I emphasized to him that they were so nice that I didn't have the heart to tell them no. "Listen; we know what time they are coming, so why don't we just shut the lights off in the house and wait until they come and go."

Mike looked at me with a frown on his face. "We are not hiding from these guys in our own house. We'll go and get pizza with the girls, and by the time we come back, they will have come and gone." I agree, thinking it was better than hiding in the dark until they're gone. So we put the coats on the girls and told them we were going for pizza, which was an unexpected treat for them.

We stayed out long enough to make sure the men coming to talk to us about the Bible would have already come. Surely they would have knocked on our door, seen that the lights were out, and figured we weren't home. We headed home, and once inside, I got the girls ready for bed. I gave them their usual kisses and hugs and walked into the living room. I was thinking, Whew, we missed the men with the Bibles. The next time they show up at my door I'll tell them, "Thank you anyway, but no thanks."

Just when we thought we were free and clear, we saw headlights pulling into the driveway. "Who could that be?" I said as I looked out the window. "Oh my goodness, it's them! The guys with the Bibles!

They are coming to the door. Quick, shut the lights off!" I screamed to Mike. He looked at me as though I was crazy. "It's too late; they know we're home. We'll just let them in, listen to what they have to say, and then tell them we are not interested."

I heard the knock on the door and took a deep breath before I opened it. Why was I so nervous? It's not as though they were going to force us to do anything. This is ridiculous. Open up the door and let them in; it's freezing out there. We greeted them at the door and invited them in. They were not the same men who had come before. I chuckled to myself.

How many of these Bible men were there? One of the men was a younger guy, and the second was at least twice his age. They apologized for being late. "We ran into some problems and didn't think we would be this late. Do you mind if we still spend some time talking with you both?"

That night we were shown in the Bible how we could know for sure that we were going to heaven. It all made sense, but with my attitude of "Don't trust anyone," I wasn't sure

I believed what they were saying. After showing me twice through Scripture that I could know for sure about my eternal destiny, they asked me if I believed that I was going to heaven.

Both times I said, "I think I have a good chance. I've never tried to purposely hurt anyone." It didn't matter that a lot of my choices in life were far from godly; it just mattered to me that I didn't purposely try to hurt anyone. I still thought that my eternal life depended on me and no one else. My husband had already seen the simplicity in what the Bible was telling him about life after death, but I wasn't so sure.

What if they are a cult? I'm still mourning Richard's death, and on top of that, his death has stirred up haunting memories of the past and how Kathy had died. I don't want to get mixed up in some wacky belief. Besides, why does the young guy keep smiling like he's so happy, and why does he talk about the power of the Holy Spirit? I watched him closely and began to conclude that he must be on some kind of drug. No one is that happy unless they are on some kind of medication.

They were so patient with me. Step by step they showed me in the Bible again how I could know about eternal life. It wasn't by chance; and if I would just believe what the Bible said, I could have assurance of eternal life. Slowly and deliberately they went through one verse at a time and let me read it.

Then the older man said, "So do you believe what the Bible says about that?"

My response was always, "Well, I believe the Bible, so if it's in the Bible, I have to believe what it says."

After going through all the verses, once again the older gentleman asked me if I thought I was on my way to heaven. I thought for a moment and then replied, "According to the Bible, no, I guess I'm not. I've depended on myself and not on what Christ has done for me."

I realized Christ could give me the peace and rest I so needed; Mike understood that also. We saw through Scripture that the life we both were living was headed down a path of destruction. Parties, booze, and all the things that go with it were destroying both of our lives, our marriage, and our family. It was at this point Mike and I bowed our heads and together asked the Lord to save us. It didn't matter if our sins were great or small, any sin required a Savior. Who would have thought that something so simple would give us something so great—the assurance of eternal life?

Attending service that day set in motion a series of events that answered many of the questions I had about life. These events were not by chance but were part of a greater plan. I was able to realize that purpose in life was not in the many material things collected or in the power we receive from achieving greatness. My purpose in life was found in the simple act of acceptance.

Salvation was offered to me like someone offering candy in an open hand and saying, "Go ahead; take it; it's free, and it's yours." I didn't have to do anything to earn salvation. I just needed to make the decision to accept it.

After that night, Mike and I began to change, definitely for the better. We began to go to church as a family and listen to a great man preach the Word of God, and with that came knowledge, and with knowledge came change. Slowly, the Lord did a mighty work in us, and I'm saying mighty because anyone who knew us would testify to how much both of us had changed. As we grew in the knowledge of Christ, our outlook on life did also. Some of the things in our past that were most damaging to us fell away. Priorities changed, and so did our hope for the future. It was as if pieces of the past that were ugly began to peel away, layer by layer. I'm not saying that overnight we became perfect human beings; we knew that wasn't going to happen now or ever, but the things we desired changed, and that was a good thing.

Our family values took a great leap forward. Connections were made with other families in the church, and our children thrived in the environment. The change in Mike and me was evident, even to our five-year-old daughter, Joscelyn, who proclaimed with a great smile one day after church, "Things are different now, aren't they, Mom and Dad?" Mike and I looked at each other and with great laughter said, "They certainly are."

My relationship with God was different; it was a personal relationship I had never had before. I knew that the Lord had a great work to do in helping me repair the pain of my past. There was a great deal for me to understand, and gently God took my hand and showed me the way.

For the first time in my life, I knew there was a place I could go to find rest, and that knowledge came just in time. I so desperately needed it. He taught me, *Come unto me, all ye that labour and are heavy laden, and I will give you rest* (Matthew 11:28). I clung to this truth, and it was about to be tested.

A CHILD IS MISSING

Of two sisters one is always the watcher,
one the dancer.

LOUISE GLUCK
*

CHAPTER EIGHTEEN

Just when I thought that after eleven years people had forgotten that November day Kathy was left in the dismal cold woods of New Hampshire, the morning headlines in the newspaper read, "Eleven Year Old Slay Case Of Girl, 13, Open Again."

Her picture stared at me from the front page, and the memories came through like an open floodgate. Not halfway open, not three-quarters open, but as wide as the gates could stretch, allowing the force of the water to bring me to my knees and engulf me. As I tumbled, my body was slammed up against the rocks, bringing blood to the surface. There, you've done it; the old wounds are opening once again, deep and bleeding.

Here we go again—interviews, questioning, confronting the pain as if it were yesterday. Why now? Has some new evidence come in? Do they have someone they are about to arrest? How will they treat us this time? Will it be with compassion or as before, forcefully pushing through, full steam ahead, not taking into consideration that to us her death seems like yesterday? How will my parents bear going through round two? Will they be able to survive going through all the details of her murder again?

As much as we wanted the case to be solved and whoever was involved to be brought to justice, there was one fact that was evident: the hurt would once again be great. There would be a great gulf of pain for my parents, my siblings, and me, and there was no escaping it. No short cut to take down an easier road.

The difference for me this time was that I had a real relationship with God. I now knew things about Him I had never known before. I looked up into the heavens, and my eyes told God the story. I didn't need to speak a word to Him. He knew the pain and fear I felt, and the strength I was going to need to talk about the past. Since I had become closer to Him, I had developed a way to ease the pain brought on by my sister's and brother's deaths. I used to think of others who had gone through worse things than I had and prayed for them. This time I thought of my Savior and what He did for me. Beaten and bruised, He hung on the cross for me. Unjustly accused but willing to go just so that *whosoever believeth in him should not perish, but have eternal life* (John 3:15). I was unworthy and undeserving, but He did it anyway. This is what I thought about as I prepared myself for yet another round of painful memories.

I really didn't know if my parents had it in them to go through another round of torture. Kathy's death had certainly taken a toll on them, as individuals and as a couple. I remember the day my mom sat me down and told me that they could no longer be married to each other. I immediately started to cry. I knew things were not good for them, but I still had hoped it could be worked out.

"Karen, we just can't stay married any longer. I can't go on living like this," Mom told me. I had nothing to say, just tears that revealed how sad I was for both of them. They ended up getting the divorce, but they never did let go of each other. For a time after the divorce, my dad actually lived with us because he had nowhere else to go. They stayed in separate rooms when they slept, but in every other way it seemed like nothing had changed.

Eventually Dad did get his own place, but they still spent all their days together. They didn't know how to cope with the death of Kathy. When they looked at each other, they saw her, and it was a constant reminder of their anguish. As their child, I wished for it to be different. I wanted them to fall in love again and ease each other's pain. But that wasn't to be; they were torn, and so was I.

I wanted to tell her that I loved her, and not in the complicated way I loved our parents, but in a simple way I never had to think about. I loved her like breathing.

BRENNA YOVANOFF
*

CHAPTER NINETEEN

Earl and Lucielle Gloddy

Earl Gloddy in uniform

Kathy in 1964

Kathy in 1966

Kathy in 1967

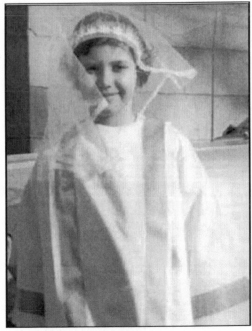

Kathy's first communion

Kathy's first school dance

Kathy at a pumpkin carving contest

Kathy in 1971, the last picture taken of her

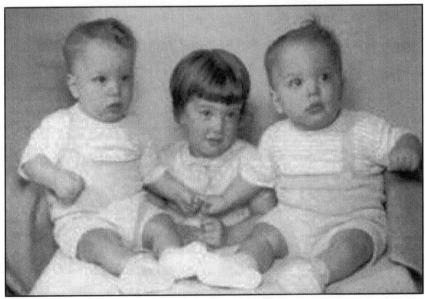

Richard, Ann, and Roger

Richard, Ann, and Roger on Easter

Ann Gloddy

Janet Gloddy

Karen Gloddy

Richard, Roger, Ann, Janet, Karen, and Kathy on Easter

Roger, Richard, Lucielle, Earl, Ann, Karen, Kathy, and Janet

Twins Roger and Richard

Gloddy house on East High Street in Franklin, New Hampshire

Bell's Variety where Kathy bought an ice cream
sandwich and Potato Sticks, two of her favorite things.

Main Street of Franklin going to Franklin High School

Franklin High School where Kathy was
seen peering into the cafeteria window

The lawn Kathy crossed heading toward the bridge where
she was last seen. This was heading away from home.

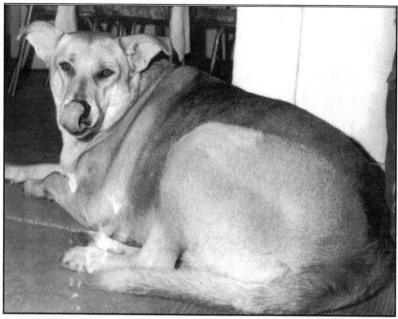

Tasha, Kathy's dog, who was with her the night she went
missing. He returned home without her in a frantic state.

Webster Road, the road I had a strong feeling to go up when
my dad and I were searching for Kathy that night. The next
day she was found murdered in the woods on that road.

Franklin Falls Dam. Kathy's friend said she might be hiding there.
Janet and I told police and helped them search, but Kathy wasn't there.

City Hall, where the police station stood in 1971.

Entrance to the police station. Janet and I entered that door
many times to speak with the police about Kathy's murder.

Janet and me with the poster Kathy was working on before
she was killed. It was about love. Photo: Fosters Newspaper

Kathy's gravestone.

CHAPTER TWENTY

As I talked to the detective working on the case, he brought up a familiar name. When this man's name was mentioned, a flashback of the incident that happened years before came to mind. "I know who he is. He and his wife rented the upstairs apartment from my parents. I did some babysitting for them in my teens. Why are you asking about him now? I don't remember his name being brought up in 1971 during the original investigation." The detective told me he was a person of interest and that they would like to speak to me about him. We agreed on a time to meet at the police station the following day.

All those years went by and I told no one, never shared it with the police. It was an embarrassing moment that I wanted to keep to myself. I didn't know this man's background and thought that it was an isolated occurrence involving me, so I decided to keep it a secret. People might question why a child would not tell an adult about something like this, but how does a person bring up a subject like that? Even today it's not easy to talk about, and in 1971 the subject of molestation or rape was something that was rarely discussed. So it became my secret for all those years until his name was brought up during the reactivation of Kathy's murder.

That night I told Mike that the police wanted to talk to me about the man who had lived upstairs from us. After confiding in Mike about what had happened, I explained that he was the first one I had ever told. Although it was hard to tell him, it actually felt good to finally tell someone.

Mike was concerned about the appointment I had with the detective. He was worried about the memories that would resurface for me because of the investigation. "Karen, you don't need to do this. Don't let them make you do anything you don't want to do. Telling them what you told me most likely doesn't have anything to do with Kathy's death."

I thought it was sweet that he was so concerned, but I expressed to him that I felt it important since the man's name was mentioned. Maybe he did have something to do with Kathy's disappearance and murder. I knew that sometimes in an old case like this, new evidence or information could be revealed and it might be just the right piece to bring it to a conclusion. There could be one little thing that someone remembered—a person said this, did this, went there, or knew him—and it could make a difference.

I woke up the next morning with an anxiety and nervousness that I hadn't had for some time. Some of the same feelings I had years ago began to creep back—wondering what had happened to her, walking through the steps of that night she went missing. Was something overlooked? The mind can be so cruel sometimes, not a kind and friendly place. So many things could have turned out differently if we had the ability to alter sections of time.

When I began to imagine how horrified she must have been, it broke my heart. Did she know her fate was death? Did she suffer? I imagined her suffering and tried to play out a different scenario in my head. Maybe she died instantly from a blow to the head, abdomen, or some other part of the body. But I knew she was beaten, so in reality, I knew that she fought for her life. She didn't give up easily; the autopsy proved that. Step by step I played it out, over and over again.

Enormous guilt surfaced as I considered that he may have had something to do with Kathy's death. Why didn't the detectives bring up his name to me in 1971? I might have connected what happened to me with what had happened to her.

Were there others? Could he have hurt other girls just like me? I knew I was doing the right thing by going to the police station and speaking with them, but it wasn't easy. It was difficult talking to my husband about it, never mind talking to men I didn't know. Earnestly I prayed, "God, give me strength and wisdom and remembrance of anything that might be important."

As I headed to the police station, I reviewed the events of that day. I narrowly escaped being raped by a man who possibly had something to do with Kathy's murder. To be raped or have an attempt made on you is a vile act, and it affects you for the rest of your life. Life would be so much easier if there were a giant eraser you could push back and forth over the mind to get rid of things you don't want to remember.

I walked into the police station and waited for them to call my name. As I entered the room, two men were there. One sat at a desk, and the other stood in the corner. He was tall and skinny and kept his arms folded across his chest. He stood in that corner the whole time I was there, without any expression on his face. The man at the desk was the one who did the talking. He proceeded without much expression on his face either.

Maybe this is what happens to people when they work on cases like this; they have to put up some kind of wall so they can deal with the things they see and talk about. It didn't make me feel very comfortable, but I understood why they did it. I definitely had put up my own walls over the years to deal with the pain that came my way.

The detective looked at me as he placed a recording device on the desk. "I would like to record our interview, if you don't mind." He pressed the button on the recorder. "Just go ahead whenever you are ready."

Taking a deep breath, I began to speak.

I started to tell them about the incident upstairs at my old house on East High Street. I didn't get very far when tears filled my eyes. I apologized, and he told me not to worry about it.

"Just take your time," he said.

With a heavy sigh, I continued, "I have never told anyone about this. I just told my husband for the first time the other day."

Again he said, "Just take your time and don't worry about it." I found comfort in those words; not just in the words, but in the way he said them. He truly sounded sympathetic, and I could sense he was trying to make this interview as easy for me as possible.

I told him everything I could remember about the man who rented the apartment upstairs, and about what happened the day I babysat—from the attempt to how I ran away. I told him that I babysat for the man one more time, but I never saw him or his family after that night and suspected that they must have moved out of Franklin. I mentioned that his name was never brought up in the original investigation; and that if it had, I would have said something.

I was totally drained after that testimony. I cried off and on through the entire interview and was certainly relieved to be finished. I was extremely thankful that I didn't need to keep it to myself anymore, and it gave me hope that maybe in some small way I had helped point them down the right path to find Kathy's murderer.

How could she just leave me here to live without
her? I miss her so much. I love her. I want her to
grow up and become who she was meant
to be. I wanted her to grow up with me.

AVA DELLAIRA
*

CHAPTER TWENTY-ONE

Far too many times the punishment for such a horrendous crime is way too lenient. So often what the victim goes through is more severe than the punishment given to the person who actually committed the crime. The emotional trauma for the victim and the victim's family goes on for years, probably for the rest of their lives. The whole family goes through the torment of what has been done to the person they love. To think that what happened to you might have happened to others is hard to absorb. To know that in many cases, whoever committed the atrocious crime is not punished accordingly and is free to do it again is mind-boggling.

I honestly didn't know how law enforcement dealt with the repeat offenders who committed unspeakable crimes upon children. They were caught and brought to trial, only to serve a minimal sentence and be let out on the streets to begin the cycle all over again. I went to the Lord and asked, "Why can't You just protect the children? Please, Lord, I beg You to at least protect the children."

Although my faith had grown tremendously over the last few years, I didn't always possess a constant state of peace and happiness. Accepting Christ as my Savior changed my life. I had a faith that I had never had before, and it brought my family down a different road than the one we had been traveling. The views I had about life, about my very existence, had changed, and it truly was because I had a God I knew loved me no matter what.

This thought was especially comforting when heartache came knocking at my door once again. When I experienced sorrow, I went back to the knowledge I had of Him and understood the truth. Even though we see the evils of this world continue, it is not of Him. He is the giver of all things good, and from the very beginning of our creation He has always wanted to have a relationship with us. We are the ones who choose to ignore Him and, because of our free will, can take the path of good or evil. Unfortunately, there are many who choose the latter.

My God is not the author of confusion or sin, and He is not to be blamed. It's much easier to blame others for our sin. So often we are like children in trouble, trying to push the blame on a sibling so there is an escape from the consequences. In the same way, when life is not what we expect or when a great injustice has been done, we tend to blame God because we know that He could have stepped in and changed the outcome.

There is no doubt in my mind that He could—He is all-powerful. But we have a will to choose right or wrong, to help or destroy, or to change the future for better or for worse. God is not the one who has changed; we have. So when the trials came and I was in an unpleasant place in the valley, I did not blame God; for I knew He was the one who loved me more than anyone else, and the proof was in His Son.

I knew that I would have fear and trust issues for the rest of my life. I prayed about this constantly. It was difficult not to live a life of being overly suspicious of others, especially men. I wondered about the motives of others and was uncomfortable taking someone's word at face value. I weighed out what they said and tried to discern if they had some ulterior motive.

One of my greatest fears was for my girls. With the addition of Nicole in 1982, I now had three daughters, and I kept them very close to me. It was a fine line between making sure that they were protected but not suffocated, between making them aware of the dangers in the world but not putting so many fears in them that they were frightened of everyone. I realized that no matter how much I instructed them to be careful, a situation could occur that might make them forget everything they were taught. Children don't see the dangers in situations as adults do and really can't imagine that anyone would ever hurt them. I hated that we had to live like that, but that's just the way life was then. If a child in a small community could walk to the store one night in 1971 and never come home, it was even more likely to happen in 1983.

Awareness of my surroundings stayed in a heightened state. Even today, when I feel something is suspicious, especially when it comes to children, I am not afraid to speak up. When a child is crying hysterically and someone is dragging them to a car, it sends me into protective mode. I want to make sure they are okay and with the person they should be with. Once I was in a store and heard the words, "Code Adam." It sent shivers up and down my spine, and I instantly started scanning the area to see if there was anything out of the ordinary going on. I read the book on little Adam Walsh, and it broke my heart. Even now I ache with memories of the past when I hear about a child who is missing. I guess my heart will always feel that way.

CHAPTER TWENTY-TWO

I can understand why someone wouldn't want to go forward and press charges against a criminal who has violated them. I know that feeling of secrecy and of not wanting anyone to know what happened to you and just wanting to forget it.

Mike and I had discussions about why someone wouldn't come forward and reveal a criminal in a sexual case, or why they wouldn't agree to testify against them. He couldn't understand why a person who was raped wouldn't come forward and tell someone, but I knew that he didn't understand that it's about not wanting to relive the pain and the humiliation of it all. Even though society today promotes coming forward when a rape occurs—and there is more help for those who do—I believe that many don't come forward. If they are children or teenagers, they are more likely to keep it a secret. Unless you've experienced the humiliation and shame, you may not understand what I am talking about. But for those who have, no matter how often they are encouraged to tell someone, the tendency is to live with the secret.

I went through life trying to suppress the violation that had been done to me. The sad thing is that keeping it a secret doesn't stop the wicked person who committed the crime from hurting someone else in the same devastating way. I learned from the new investigation of Kathy's murder that the man in question had a history of violating young girls. Before Kathy was killed, he had served time in the New Hampshire state prison.

I was only thirteen when this man sexually assaulted me. At the time I convinced myself that I was his only victim, but with this new information I realized that was not the case. From that moment on I understood that keeping my secret was more damaging than confiding in someone and exposing him for the evil person he was.

If you are reading this and a crime has been committed against you, there is help for you. There are people who care deeply that you have been hurt; and if one person won't listen, tell someone else. Even in our small community, people could have helped me deal with my assault, but I didn't know who to turn to. It should never be that way; every child should know a person they can confide in if a similar thing happens to them.

There isn't any town, city, or small neighborhood that goes untouched by the wickedness of sexual assault. In 1971, some people knew who the sexual predators were in our small community, but no one spoke up to protect the children; it was easier to keep it all a secret.

We waited patiently for someone to have the courage to come forward with the information needed to help solve Kathy's murder. Even if they thought it wasn't important, it might be what the police needed to make an arrest, to give my family closure, and to give Kathy justice. Maybe they could save another innocent victim from a brutal death and spare a family from the destructive forces of such a crime.

The detective asked me if I could remember the house where Kathy bought fireworks for the Fourth of July. "Oh yes, I remember exactly where it is, and I can take you there."

On the Fourth of July, Kathy and I were talking about how disappointed we were because we didn't have any fireworks. Kathy told me she knew a man who had some if Mom would agree to drive us to his house. We drove up to a house; Kathy got out and seemed to know exactly where to go. She bypassed the front door and walked down a narrow sidewalk to the back of the house. I didn't remember her bringing this man up in any conversations, so I wondered how she knew him.

Many of Kathy's poems reflected her interest in the war, and she was concerned about Roger, who was stationed in Germany. This man was given a hero's welcome when he came back to Franklin after serving his country as a Green Beret, but I didn't really pay much attention to the whole ordeal. Maybe she had been curious about his military career. Several minutes later she came out with a small armful of fireworks. We were both very excited that we had some fireworks to light for the festivities that night.

The detectives took a recorder, and we got into a police car. I sat in the backseat of the car as they drove toward the Franklin hospital. This was the same hospital where Kathy's autopsy was done.

I instructed the officers to continue down the road. We passed the hospital on the left, and I intently watched the street signs. "Take this left," I told them.

As soon as we took the left, I knew it was the wrong street. "Oh, I remember that his street was a dead-end street. This is the wrong street; it's the street before this one." They immediately turned around and headed back the way we had come.

We reached the top of the street, and I said, "Take a right here, and then take the next right."

They followed my instructions and made the turns. "This is it, this is the street." I pointed to my left. "That's his house."

"Are you sure?" they said.

"I'm positive. I remember being here."

They spoke into the recorder, "The address of the house is 30 South Sulloway Street."

"Now tell us how Kathy approached the house." I looked at the house in front of me and my imagination brought me back. I could almost see her walking toward the house.

"She walked down the sidewalk and went around to the back of the house; at that point she wasn't visible. It wasn't long before she came back around and walked up the sidewalk to the car with the fireworks in her hands."

Again, they spoke into the recorder, "Make note that Kathy went to the back of the house and did not enter the front door. This implies that she knew there was a back door in which to enter the house." They asked me if she had ever been there before, and how she knew to go to the back of the house instead of using the front door. "I don't know. I can't even tell you if she'd ever been there before." I wished I could have helped them more, but facts were facts: she had never spoken to me about him. I never had a conversation with her about how she knew him or how she knew he had fireworks to purchase.

Maybe she knew him from the Franklin Recreation Center; he was there on a regular basis. Many of us went there to play games and hang out together. It was within walking distance from our home, and it wasn't unusual to go there. A lot of neighborhood kids spent time at the center, especially if they were into sports. It was a safe place to hang out, and the activities kept us busy.

There are certain things we owe our little sisters.

CLAIRE HENNESSY
*

CHAPTER TWENTY-THREE

As the investigation continued, it was very hard on my mom and dad. They waited every day for news that someone had been charged with the murder of their little girl. The detectives confided in Janet and me most of the time because they felt it was too much of a strain on my parents. They wanted to question them as little as possible, knowing that both of them were very fragile when it came to talking about Kathy's murder. I continually made myself available to detectives, and so did Janet; it didn't matter what they needed to talk to us about. As painful as the memories were, both of us would do anything to help.

I received a phone call one day and was asked if I could come to the police station and answer some more questions. They wanted to speak with me again about the man who rented the upstairs apartment from my parents. I entered the police station through a door that was becoming familiar to me. The detective approached me, shook my hand, and thanked me for coming in. We walked to his office, where

I knew I would have to reminisce about a past I wanted to forget. I sat down and thought I would have to excuse myself to find a bathroom because of the nausea I felt building.

We went over some of the previous testimony I had given him. The detective told me that when he did some research on this man, he found out that he was supposed to have been in prison for statutory rape of a young girl in the area at the time Kathy had been murdered. As I learned more about him and his reputation, in my mind I began to refer to him as "the evil man."

The detective looked up from the papers on his desk and said, "I'm going to call right now and see if he was in prison at the time Kathy was murdered. That's where he was supposed to be, but I want to make sure of his release date."

I watched as he dialed the prison's number. He informed the person on the other end that he was inquiring about a prisoner from 1971. "I would like to know his sentence and his release date." He gave them the prisoner's full name, and we sat there waiting for them to get the information.

I watched him as he asked them to verify again the date he had been given. I followed his pen as he wrote it down on a piece of paper, and as he hung up the phone he looked at me. The shock on his face was obvious. "He was out; he wasn't in prison at all. He was walking around a free man when your sister was killed. He was supposed to have served a longer sentence for what he had done to a young girl in the area, but they let him out early."

My jaw dropped. "How could they not have checked that back in 1971?" I exclaimed. "Why would they take it for granted that he was in prison? Shouldn't they have verified that information?"

I found out that he had been on the original suspect list in 1971, but police had taken him off because he supposedly was in prison at the time of the murder. Maybe that's why I don't remember his name ever coming up in the original investigation. He knew our family, he knew her, and he made an attempt on me. He had a reputation we didn't know about, and he was out when Kathy was murdered.

Such a simple thing—a phone call could have made a difference in how they looked at the information they had and maybe sent them in a different direction. That didn't mean the other suspects were innocent, but I believe with all my heart now that the person in question was involved. Why didn't they check to make sure he was in prison? They took it for granted that he was. What else did they take for granted? What other information were they careless with? An important suspect had slipped through the cracks, someone who definitely had the potential to rape and kill, and it was evident that the detective sitting in front of me was visibly upset. He had an expression of disbelief on his face as he came to grips with what he had been told. Again I thought, How could someone not take the time to make a simple phone call and verify the information they had on this man? Even I knew that was a huge mistake, and that this man could be the key to splitting this case wide open.

The detective continued to sit there in disbelief. I think he forgot I was in the same room with him. He began to have a conversation with himself, processing the information that was racing through his mind. I sat there listening to the whole conversation. Was I supposed to try to answer some of the questions he was asking himself? Suddenly he looked at me with regret, as if apologizing, and repeated what I already knew—that this suspect had not been in prison at the time of Kathy's murder. What a grave mistake for someone to make.

In disbelief, I said, "We know that some of his friends were not ideal citizens. You can't tell me that one of them doesn't know what happened. They must have some information that could be valuable to this case. Why wouldn't they be willing to help, unless, of course, they could be implicated in some way? Maybe they were there when it happened or helped to hide evidence."

My head was swimming with all the unknowns. I made eye contact with the detective and could tell that he was sympathetic. Even though this case was an investigation to him, I could see that he had a deep desire to solve it and bring closure to my family, and most importantly, bring justice to Kathy.

Once the detective knew that this man had been released from prison early, he extensively researched his background. It wasn't pretty; not only did this man serve prison time for statutory rape of a young girl in the area, but he should have been arrested for many more. The new information revealed that this girl was not the only one in the area he had raped, but she was the only one whose parents decided to press charges against him. I said a prayer for them and their daughter—what a courageous thing for them to do.

It was mentioned that there had been a number of girls who could have charged him with the same crime and helped send him away to prison, but the parents of these girls decided not to press charges. I could understand why they wouldn't, and I certainly didn't blame them. What a horrible thing to put your daughter through after she's been through so much already. I'm sure that deciding to press charges and bring this man to trial was a hard-fought battle for this family. It would be for my family. Their daughter would have to reveal step by step what had been done to her, reliving a pain she would rather forget. Not only that, but she would have to speak of it in front of the man who took something from her she wasn't willing to give. In testifying, she would have to see this man's face in the courtroom. The torment would continue for her and her family, throughout the trial and well into the future.

I know that my experience with him was probably not even close to what she experienced, but I do know that telling the detectives about it was physically and emotionally draining. And he left scars on me that I too carried around like his other victims.

The conversation between the detective and me focused in on the character of this man who brought more pain to others than I ever could have imagined. He told me that a profiler from Vermont had offered his services. He hoped that he might help solve Kathy's murder. "I don't know if you realize what profilers charge for doing this kind of work," the detective said, "but they are very expensive. This particular profiler has helped to bring justice to other families in unsolved murders, and he's offered his services for free." I didn't know much about profilers, so he explained to me that a profiler is trained to look at details in a murder and understand some of the motives and methods of a criminal.

Profilers look at what happened to the body during the crime. They can give you an idea of how the killer thinks, their character traits, or even what they might do for a living. There are many things they look at—they will review photos, the crime scene, how violent the crime was. They can be a crucial tool for detectives on a case. They give the investigators some direction, especially when some of the details fit a person on the suspect list.

CHAPTER TWENTY-FOUR

The reopening of Kathy's murder did present new testimony, new evidence, and more pieces to place in the puzzle. The detective informed me that the profiler in Kathy's case believed that the person involved or someone in his family possibly had medical problems with their feet.

As I listened to this man give me details, I thought, That's a strange thing to say. How would a person understand something like that? It was certain that any ordinary person would not have come to that conclusion. We did know that all her clothing had been taken except for her socks. Why was that? That was something I and others in my family had thought about; it was peculiar. That image always tormented me. It was a difficult thing to envision—her lying there in the woods, in the cold, dark night, with only her socks on. The image still haunts me.

I am thankful to profilers and all those in law enforcement whose goal is to bring justice to the victims and the families who loved them.

They give those who are left behind some closure about what had happened. The men and women who work on cases like Kathy's try to fill a small part of the hole left in our hearts, an emptiness caused by someone who didn't see the value in another person's life. I'm thankful for the people who have worked on Kathy's case, for those who have truly cared about what happened to her. I know there have been some that haven't; to them it's just a job. Some of the attitudes have been, "If it's solved, great; and if it's not, oh well." To those who had that attitude, all I can say is, I hope you will never face the horror of having one of your children taken from you in such an appalling way.

I cling to the fact that there are some who still care, because let me tell you, a family knows when it's genuine and the person's heart is in the right place. We can see the honesty and passion you have in laying to rest the unknown. I could see this passion in the detective I was speaking to and thanked God for him.

He looked me in the eye and said, "I eat, drink, and sleep this case. Even if the investigation slows down and I'm told not to spend as much time on this case, I'm not going to give up. I'll work on it in my own time if I have to. Someday, somewhere down the road, this guy is going to mess up. Something will come out, and we'll get him." The spark of hope was ignited, and I felt that things were once again going in the right direction. Even though this was his job, my heart was full of gratitude for the desire he had to solve her murder. I thanked the Lord for this man and those like him, for the ones who have passion and desire to fight for what's right and seek justice for those who cannot find it on their own.

Within the first year of the reactivation of the case, a reporter contacted my mom looking to do a story. He wanted to talk about any updates or progress being made in the investigation. That day I received a phone call from my mom. "Can you come over today? There is a reporter coming who wants to do a story on the investigation. He would like to take a picture of me with you and Janet to put in the article. He wants to ask some questions about the case and how the family is dealing with the reopening."

Although I didn't want to do it, I could hear in her voice that it was important. "Okay, Mom. I'll be over in a few minutes." I put the girls in the car and headed to my mom's apartment to do yet another interview.

While the reporter questioned us about how the family was dealing with the reopening of Kathy's case, Mom began to cry. I wished she hadn't agreed to give this man an interview; I hated to see her this way. We knew as a family that the media could actually help to keep an investigation up front in people's minds. Even though none of us wanted to give an interview, we knew it was important. It's easy to forget the tragedy a family faces when you're not directly involved. It's news one day, and a few days later, it's forgotten; but it is never forgotten by the family.

As he was finishing the interview, he mentioned that he wanted to have a story ready to go because he was told there might be a break in the case, maybe an arrest coming soon. We sat there in shock because none of us had received any news that there was a possibility of that happening. "How do you know that?" I asked.

"I can't give you any information on where that tip came from," he said. He took pictures of us holding Kathy's picture, the one used in most of the articles that had been done in the past. It was the last picture taken of her from St. Mary's School. She looked so sad in it. After her death, I wondered if indeed she was sad about something. She had a beautiful smile, and I wish the last picture taken of her was with the smile I remembered.

After the photos were taken, the reporter thanked us for our time and was on his way to his next story, while we were left behind to sift through the wreckage of memories he stirred within us.

Later, I called the detective in Franklin. "A journalist was at my mom's apartment asking questions and taking pictures for a story. He heard that some important information may be released to the press soon. He also said there was a strong possibility that an arrest was going to be made in Kathy's case. He received this information from a reliable source but wouldn't tell us who it was. He sounded pretty sure of himself. No one told us anything about a possible arrest. Do you have new information?"

He said there wasn't anything he could tell me and, according to him, there was nothing new to give us. "I spoke with the man doing the interview, and nothing is going to be printed in the newspaper at this time. We don't need anyone messing up this investigation after all the work we've done," he said.

The whole incident baffled me. Why would a journalist come to my mom's apartment and want to do an interview and take pictures? There had to have been a reason why he thought an arrest might be made. It was a little suspicious that the journalist seemed to know that something was about to happen and also suspicious that the detective wasn't willing to give us any information. Was there a break in the case that he wasn't willing to tell us about? Why didn't they keep us more informed? Without information, our minds created imaginary scenarios that produced unnecessary worry.

I love you with everything I am. For so long,
I just wanted to be like you. But I had to figure
out that I am someone too, and now I carry
you, your heart with mine, everywhere I go.

AVA DLLAIRA
*

CHAPTER TWENTY-FIVE

Another conversation I had with the detective revealed to me his passion to solve the mystery of Kathy's murder. We began talking about some details of the case. He flipped through the papers in front of him and started to speak as though I wasn't in the room. I sat quietly while he gave me new information. "We are hot on the trail and so close to solving this case. There is just one more thing we need to tie it all together." As I listened to him, I felt for the first time that maybe, just maybe, the case was going to be solved. He told me that a meeting was held to discuss if they should make a deal with the person they wanted to arrest, but they decided against it. It sounded as though he was instrumental in the decision not to proceed with the deal.

"I want to get this person for all he did to her; we have time. There is no statute of limitations on a murder case. She was not only beaten and raped; she was run over. Not once, but four times, to make sure she was dead." He took for granted that I knew this information. I considered that maybe he had forgotten I was in the room.

With the transcript in front of him, he proceeded to read a portion of it to me. It was a statement that someone had made during an interview. This person implied that it was Kathy's fault for being murdered because she should have been home where she belonged that night. He implied that if she was, none of this would have happened. I was stunned by the comment and sat there with tears running down my face, not saying a word.

Most of the things he was saying I had never heard before. I didn't know she had been run over a number of times. My head was swimming with thoughts and visions, horrible visions. I felt numb, but my mind was racing with all that he told me. I tried to stop my mind, but it was no use; it was out of my control. I saw her naked body lying there on the ground; broken, bruised and lifeless. I imagined the pain or terror she must have endured before her death and prayed that she had not been alive when the car passed over her four times. My heart cried out to God to make the images stop; the visions were unbearable. And although I looked calm sitting there, I wanted to scream and throw things. I wanted the person who had done this to her to taste the pain she went through, and anyone involved to suffer horribly through the rest of their life. And what did I want for my family and me? I wanted relief from the torment, the pain, and suffering that we endured from knowing all that had happened to her.

The detective looked up from his papers and turned his head to look at me. He said, "Oh, I'm so sorry. Are you okay?" I opened my mouth to speak, and at first nothing came out. Then I responded with, "That's okay; I'm all right." I wasn't all right. I was in shock. The images flooded my mind, and there wasn't a way to turn it off. It's amazing the things we can hide from someone when we don't want them to see the emotions we are feeling inside. I had become an expert at it.

I was driving away from the police station when the tears came rolling down my cheeks. There wasn't any way to control the sobbing, and from that point on until I got home I was in a terrible state of mind. As I approached the driveway, I chanted over and over to myself, "Stop! I don't want to see these images or think about this anymore." I held on to the steering wheel, trying to get composure before I entered the house and had to face my family. I didn't want Mike or the girls to see me this way. I took a deep breath and told myself to be strong, to be brave, and I whispered a little prayer: "Help me, God."

I was physically and emotionally drained and wanted to go straight to bed. I felt I could have slept for days, but I knew that I couldn't. As I had done so many times before, I pushed on and tried to cling to the fact that I had a family I loved dearly, and they loved me back. I entered into the ritual that had become part of my life during great times of trial, times when I felt that I might slip off the edge and just keep falling. I would make a list, a list that contained whatever was important to me in life—people and things I counted as blessings.

I was thankful for my husband and my children, the love I had for them and the love they had for me. Mike worked hard to provide for us, and even though there were times when things were tight financially, we always had everything we needed and then some. God took care of all our needs and most times gave us much more.

We made a decision early on that I would stay home with the girls and not work. Both of us felt that it was important for one parent to be at home, even if it meant sacrificing material things. I was overwhelmed by the love Mike had developed for the girls and me since accepting Christ as his Savior three years ago.

It wasn't like that the first five years of our marriage. We had definitely built our relationship on sandy ground, shifting here and there and headed in the wrong direction. After we began to make Christ the center of our marriage, it took on a stability that only could have come from the Solid Rock it was built upon.

My outlook on life and what I considered to be blessings had changed. That's when the "list" became more important to me. The list of thankfulness, thankful that God had changed the path we were taking as husband and wife, that the direction we now were taking to raise our girls was sweeter. I tried to think of everything I had been blessed with. It was a way to relieve my mind from being consumed by the horrible thoughts of Kathy on the ground, alone in the woods on a cold, wintry night.

It's peculiar how time just slips away and throws you into the future whether you're ready or not. Before you know it, days turn into months, and one day you realize that years have gone by. That's how it was for me. One day I woke up and realized that years had gone by and still no one had been charged with Kathy's murder. Even though time was slipping away since the detective told me they were close to charging someone with the crime, still nothing had been done. I vividly remember the detective holding up his fingers close together and saying, "We're this close." That gave me such hope back then, but as before, years floated on by and still no word of an arrest.

My family was living the past all over again. We waited for any information that the detectives might give us to keep hope in view. But that window of hope began to close once again, slow and painfully. Over and over in my head I would hear the detective say, "We are so close; hot on the trail. We just need one more thing to fall into place." What was that thing they were waiting for, and why couldn't they find it so we could have some closure? They always left us hanging, giving us less and less information as the years went on.

As a family, we clung to every little morsel given to us in hopes that it would help to keep the investigation active. We listened intently to everything they told us and held on to the fact that they were still trying, still cared. But when we heard nothing for the longest time, it was like a balloon had been released into the air: quite visible at first, but floating higher and higher until it finally disappears.

If I could plant a flower for every time I miss
you, I could walk through my garden forever.

ANONYMOUS
*

CHAPTER TWENTY-SIX

In 1990, my mom moved in with us. She was ill and needed care. I took certified nursing assistant classes to learn how to care for her and help her get well again. The day she moved into our home, Mike had to carry her in. She was so frail that she couldn't even walk. We gave her our bedroom downstairs so she would be close to a bathroom. The room was bright with natural sunlight, and that was important since she would be bedridden for some time. Mike and I took one of the bedrooms upstairs.

The girls lifted her spirits and helped with the task of getting her well again. Her weight had dropped to a dangerously low sixty-eight pounds, and it was a chore getting her to eat. Slowly, her weight began to climb and her strength returned. It was like feeding an infant; tablespoon by tablespoon, she began to recover. It took about a year before she was ready to move out on her own and have some independence again. During that year she had ups and downs, and I was able to talk to her about the Bible. She had heard it before, but this time she seemed to understand that even though her life had been weighed down by unfairness and cruelty, she too needed a Savior. Sometimes people who have had to endure heart-wrenching events feel that their suffering replaces their need for a Savior. But none of us are exempt from that need, and Mom finally understood that. She accepted Christ as her personal Savior in 1990.

Mom grew stronger and started to go to church. Eventually I encouraged her to find an apartment so she could be independent. She thought that I was throwing her out of our home, and I couldn't convince her otherwise. I don't know why she felt that I was pushing her out of our home, which was far from the truth. I thought she would be excited to have her own place. I tried to explain to her that I would be happy to have her stay, but that I thought it would be good for her to be on her own. I couldn't convince her that it was a suggestion and not a desire to get her out of the house. She was able to get into an apartment nearby, and as usual Janet and I checked on her regularly. Mom adjusted to living in her own apartment, and it was easier for Dad to spend more time with her. They still needed each other in many ways.

In the spring of 1991, my dad and I left the veterans' hospital in Manchester, where he was told his constant backache was nothing more than that—a backache. I went to his doctor's appointment because he had been in pain for some time, and the doctors were just giving him Motrin. I knew in my heart that something was wrong; he hadn't been himself for a while. It wasn't just the pain; he wasn't eating and was losing weight.

As the doctor examined him, I asked, "Why is his pain not going away? He doesn't want to eat, and he's been losing weight."

The doctor looked at me with disgust because I questioned him. "Listen, honey, if you had constant back pain you wouldn't want to eat either." I thought that he was rude and rather unprofessional.

I explained to him that my dad had not been himself for a while and that I really felt something else was wrong. "Could you please do some other tests to make sure it's not anything else?" He agreed to order some tests and said that they could be done in a local hospital closer to home.

On the way home we stopped at a Dunkin' Donuts to get a cup of coffee and a donut. It was one of my dad's favorite things in life. He loved a good cup of coffee and a donut to go along with it. I never saw him turn one down when it was offered to him. We sat inside, and I talked to him about the fact that it was good that the doctors were going to run more tests. "We want to make sure it's not anything else, Dad. It's not normal for you to be losing weight this way and to be in pain all the time." I watched him as he hardly touched his coffee or donut, and it was a testimony to the fact that something was wrong.

The following weeks were filled with tests, and the results were not good: he had cancer. When I heard the words "There's nothing we can do" from the doctor, I couldn't believe it. Lord, how much more do you want from me? I know You tell me in your Word that you will not give me more than I can handle; but truly, Lord, I don't think I can handle much more, and neither can my family.

When the family received the results, we were told that we should make an appointment to speak with the doctor about what treatments, if any, could be done. My dad was in a lot of pain that day, and it took all his strength to get to the doctor's office. Janet drove her car with my dad lying down in the backseat. My mom and I followed her in my car. I sat in the waiting room with Mom, Janet, Ann, and Dad, and it seemed to take forever before we finally saw the doctor.

The doctor walked in and looked at my father's chart and asked why we were all here. "We were told to make an appointment to discuss the results of my father's tests," I said. The doctor had a puzzled look on his face and exclaimed boldly, "He has cancer. You know that, don't you?"

My patience was almost at an end, but I replied with a simple, "Yes, we know that." Wow, I thought, this guy needs training on how to compassionately deal with people, and his following statement proved it: "Well, there isn't anything we can do. No treatments; he's going to die."

"We didn't know that. Someone obviously forgot to give us that information. If we had known that, we wouldn't have bothered to come," I stated, with restraint.

My dad was sitting there in pain, and this doctor just blurted out that he was going to die. It was a careless and heartless way to tell him. He made us feel like we had wasted his precious time.

Poor Dad. He was suffering, and we dragged him there for no reason at all. He asked the doctor for more pain pills, and the doctor's response was, "You should still have a small amount of medication left. I'm not going to prescribe any more right now."

We all walked out in shock. We knew he had cancer, but no one said that nothing could be done. All of us were prepared for him to go through some kind of treatments or take pills and everything would be fine. At the very least, we expected that whatever treatment they decided on would extend his life so we would have more time with him. As we walked to the cars, my dad mumbled under his breath, "I don't know why they made me come all this way if there isn't anything they can do."

I watched him get into the car and saw him cringe in pain as he tried to lie down in the backseat for the ride home. Since Dad couldn't care for himself, and Mom wasn't well enough to look after him, he was staying at Janet's house. I know he was thankful to be there, to be close to family, and to spend some time with Janet's boys, Christopher and James. They loved him, and the time they spent with him helped to keep his spirits up.

Early on in his struggle with cancer, we discussed details about his funeral. "I don't want a military funeral and don't put flowers on my grave. If you're going to leave anything, leave a cactus there."

I chuckled and couldn't imagine his reasoning for that. "Dad, why would you want a cactus left at your grave?"

Adamantly and with no hesitation, he said, "Because I've been such a prick all my life." It caught us by surprise, and we broke out in a fit of laughter.

"Dad, we are not going to put a cactus at your grave," I told him. "No matter how difficult you think you've been."

He decided to be cremated, and I struggled with that, but it was his decision. At first he had asked me to bury him in my backyard, and I told him I couldn't do that.

"What if I move? You'll be in the backyard, and I won't be able to take you with us. You'll be in someone else's backyard, and I'm sure they wouldn't appreciate that."

"Bring me to the stream down the road, then. I've always liked it there. That would be a good place to sprinkle my ashes." I thought about his request and decided it wasn't a good idea.

"Dad, I don't think people who use that for drinking water would appreciate your ashes in it." I'm sure he must have thought some of these things out, but it was as if he was randomly throwing out ideas.

In the months ahead we watched him slowly deteriorate. It was hard to see him suffer and become so frail. I always thought of him as a physically strong man. In his younger days as a soldier, he had done some boxing. Though my dad struggled after Kathy, he was a fighter. Maybe some of the fight instinct came from those early days as a boxer. Now he was failing, and I could tell after months of being in pain that he was beginning to give up the fight. I couldn't blame him.

CHAPTER TWENTY-SEVEN

In July 1992, Dad was rushed to the hospital. His kidneys began to shut down. I went to the emergency room and found him lying on a gurney in a confused state of mind. He looked terrible. I reached out to hold his hand. "I'm here, Dad. Janet and I won't leave you. We are going to get you admitted to the hospital, and the doctors will take care of you." He started to mumble random things to me; some made sense and some did not. Then I looked down at the urine bag by his bed; it was brown, and I knew that wasn't a good sign. I said, "I love you, Dad. I'm going to stay right here, and Janet and I will go upstairs with you when they admit you."

I believe he thought he was going to die that day. He was worried that he would never live to see Kathy's murder solved, that he would never see justice played out for her or for our family. He was lying there in pain, and his thoughts were on Kathy. He was worried he would die while the one who took her life still walked the streets freely.

I couldn't give him any hope. I had no comforting words to assure him that justice was right around the corner; no way to promise him that even if he died today, justice would be ours in the future. As I watched him try to get comfortable, I wished it were me instead of him. One of the most difficult things in life is watching someone you love suffer. My dad had suffered enough. "Why him, God? Why now?" Yet I knew in my heart that if it were me instead of him, he would find it unbearable to watch. He had already endured two of his children passing on before him; another would surely bring him to a place of no return.

Being a mother, I could understand how a parent would gladly take whatever pain their child was going through to spare them of the suffering. On the other end, I couldn't understand those who wouldn't. Most parents, I believe, would die for their child if they needed to. My dad would have; he would have taken Kathy's place if given the chance. I believe his last wish would have been to make sure that justice was given to his little girl.

The days spent in the hospital were long; the visits consisted of sitting by his side and encouraging him to eat. His medications began to help with the malfunctioning of his kidneys, and he started to look better and get some of his spunk back. I missed his sarcasm. His nurses were concerned because he wasn't eating and told him he would not be able to go home if he didn't start taking in some nourishment. One day I walked into his room, and he said they were going to release him soon. The nurse came in and took the food tray. "Congratulations! You finished almost half your meal."

He smiled. "Thank you." As she walked out of the room, he looked at me with a big smile on his face, which was a sign he was feeling better. It also meant he had something up his sleeve, and after he knew she was gone, he said, "Look in the garbage can." There, in the trash, was the food the nurse had just congratulated him on eating.

He burst out laughing. "She thought I ate it! I fooled her! I'm getting out of here. I don't care what they say." Though I knew it didn't benefit him at all to not eat, I had to laugh because it was like having my old dad back again.

Of course, I scolded him as best I could with the smile that was planted on my face. "Dad, it doesn't do you any good to make pretend you ate your food." But I knew it didn't matter. Just to see him laugh again, even if it was temporary, was worth the little trick he played on the nurse. It was so good to hear him laugh; not just see him smile, but to hear the laugh I remembered as a child. I missed it and tried to commit it to memory, knowing that there wouldn't be many more days to enjoy that sound.

After he left the hospital, he went to the veterans' home in Tilton. I was willing to care for Dad in my home, but circumstances didn't permit it. Roger flew in from Colorado to visit him and to take care of some family legal matters. After Dad was admitted to the Veterans Home and Roger saw that things were in order, he returned to his job and his family.

That was hard on my dad; he asked for him frequently. He would ask me when Roger was coming back to get him out of this place. He wanted to go home. It was difficult for Mom to see my dad in the condition he was in, so Ann, Janet, and I spent as much time with him as we could. Once again we were thrown together by unpleasant circumstances. Because Janet and I lived nearby, we were able to see him just about every day. We made sure to visit him in the morning and then again at night.

Periodically Janet brought Christopher and James to see their pepé, and I brought Joscelyn, Melissa, and Nicole. Ann's youngest daughter Jessica still lived at home, and at times she came with Ann to visit him. We wanted him to know that he was loved. Sometimes when people haven't met our expectations, they think that we don't value their lives. We wanted Dad to know that we did value his life and that he was important to all of us. As children we tried to make sure our parents, even with their faults, knew that we valued them. After all, are there any of us who live our lives without fault?

Cancer is cruel to the people it attacks, and also to the ones who love them. It wasn't a quick death, and I watched as he slowly lost his battle with the disease. It really wasn't a battle. It was more like a waiting period—watching life turn the corner toward death. He continued to lose weight because he wasn't eating. Nourishment came from what little fluids he labored to take in through a straw. When his strength was gone and death's door was beginning to open, the staff put him in a private room so we could be with him whenever we wanted.

After they got him settled, I walked into the room and noticed the mirror had a sheet over it. With a puzzled look on my face, I pointed to it and asked Ann, "Why is this sheet over the mirror?"

Ann whispered so Dad couldn't hear, "They brought Dad in, and he saw his reflection in the mirror. He asked, 'Who is that man in the mirror? I don't know him.'"

My sisters covered it up so he wouldn't have to see the man that he'd become.

He asked to see pictures of himself when he was in uniform and serving his country. He wanted to remember a time when he was young, standing tall and proud. Janet found some pictures of him taken many years ago in his uniform and brought them so he could see what he looked like. The pictures of him healthy and young erased the image of the man he saw earlier in the mirror.

That moment when you actually feel
the pain in your chest from seeing
or hearing what breaks your heart.

AUTHOR UNKNOWN
*

CHAPTER TWENTY-EIGHT

One night I sat with Dad and worked on a cross-stitch project while he slept. Off and on he would wake up and talk to me a little. If there had been a recliner or a more comfortable chair in his room, it might have been easier for all of us to sit with him for long periods of time. It was close to midnight when I told him I had to go. "Dad," I whispered, "I'll be back in the morning to see you. I need to go home and get some sleep."

"No," he said. "Don't go. Can't you stay? I can't sleep when you're gone." I was exhausted; the days were long, and the nights even longer. I was trying to take care of my family and spend as much time with my dad as possible. Ann and Janet did, too. We were all pretty tired. Mom visited less frequently as his condition got worse. It was difficult for her to see him like that, especially at the end. Again, I promised him I would be back as soon as the kids were off to school in the morning. "Okay," he said. I walked out feeling guilty about leaving, but I knew if I didn't get some sleep, I wasn't going to be good for anything.

First thing in the morning as promised, I was back in his room. When he saw me he looked relieved. "Oh good, you're here. I waited all night for you to come." My heart ached and I thought, I should have stayed on the floor. Why didn't I just stay on the floor? I felt so bad.

"I'm sorry, Dad. I came as soon as I could." I pulled up the chair that had become familiar and sat in it once again and held his hand. "Go to sleep, Dad. I'm here. Get some rest, okay?"

He smiled and drifted off to sleep. I sat with him for a few hours, went home and got some lunch, took care of some family duties, and was back after dinner to sit with him for a few more hours. When I wasn't there, Janet would stay with him. We tried to be there as much as possible. On the weekends, Ann would come from Rochester to give us support and to visit with him too.

We were all exhausted from the long days and the emotional strain of watching Dad drift closer to the day he would leave us forever. One night we were in his room just talking about old times and trying to get some relief from the reality that he was dying. I began to tell Ann a funny story of someone I had dealt with as a counselor for a teen camp. She assumed that the story was about a girl around ten years old, and as she took a sip of her coffee, I told her it was a college student. She nearly choked, and coffee came spurting out of her nose. All three of us were so exhausted that we couldn't contain our laughter and had to leave my father's room.

It was the first lighthearted moment we had in some time. Even though my dad wasn't speaking or responding much anymore, I wondered if he could hear our laughs. Did it bring him back to when his little girls giggled and danced in the sunlight? Did it bring him joy to hear his three girls laugh again? During this time we bonded as sisters, and I knew that no matter what, we had been through tough times before, and together we would overcome once again.

One night as I was getting ready to leave, Dad called me closer so he could whisper in my ear. I bent over and put my ear near his mouth. "Karen, I want you to do something for me."

"What, Dad? What do you need?"

"I want you to kill me," he said as if it was a normal request of his daughter. I looked at him with sadness and said, "Dad, I can't do that." I was stunned that he asked me to do such a thing. With pleading eyes, he spoke softly, "It's okay, Karen. You can, and it won't hurt. Just cut my wrist, and it will be quick." With this, he made a motion across his wrist as if a knife was passing over it.

"Dad, you know I can't do that. It would be wrong." Then, with an expression of disappointment, he said to me, "But why? You're my daughter." With that, I burst into tears. There was sympathy in my voice as I said, "I'm sorry, Dad. I love you, but I just can't do something like that." I felt that I had let him down, that his daughter whom he loved and would have protected if necessary had failed him when he needed her most. I knew it was an impossible thing for me to carry out, but the feeling of betraying him was great, and the guilt I felt because of it was unexpected.

I stayed and held his hand for a while, and when it was time for me to leave, I gave him a kiss on the cheek and said, "I love you, Dad."

He turned his face from me. When I walked out of the room, I broke down and sobbed uncontrollably.

The nurse at the desk approached me, "Can I do anything to help you?" I told her what had happened, and with an understanding heart she told me she knew exactly what I was talking about.

"My dad had cancer, and he asked me to do the same thing. It's very common for people with cancer to ask one of their family members to take their life. They want the pain to end." She hugged me and said she was sorry for the hurt my family was feeling.

With tears running down my face, I hugged her back and said, "Thank you for understanding and sharing that with me. I felt so guilty that I couldn't do what he asked of me."

With a tender voice she said to me, "I know. If you ever need to talk to someone, let me know." It was one of the few times someone reached out to us.

My dad's request seemed so cruel. How could he ask his daughter to do such a thing? And then make me feel like I had let him down because I refused to fulfill his last request? It devastated me. After the conversation with the nurse, I realized it was a common request. I was able to process what had just happened and come to grips with the guilt I was feeling. I realized that he just wanted it to be over, and I had to agree that if I was in his place, I would want it to be over too.

As I lay in bed that night, I prayed, "Please, Lord, don't let him suffer much longer. But before he goes, let him know You as I know You." Dad didn't yet have the security of knowing his final destination.

I explained to him that the Bible reveals to us how we can know for sure. In the past, I had discussions with him about this very subject. We don't need to guess or wonder about it.

The concept of salvation being free to all who ask for it was hard for him to understand. Like so many others, he based salvation on works—what he had done or didn't do in his life. He knew he fell short of what a Holy God would want. He told me that he couldn't possibly be saved and spend eternity in heaven because of the things he had done, "especially in the war." He lived with no hope of heaven.

I've felt broken almost beyond repair at several points in my life — but I am slowly learning (very slowly) how to stop piecing myself together and allow the Great Physician to do His mending. And I can tell you those stitches are more beautiful and lasting than anything I was ever able to do.

RUTHIE DEAN
*

CHAPTER TWENTY-NINE

The weeks ahead were difficult for all of us. Dad was failing. He wasn't eating and his fluid intake was limited. As I entered his room for one of our visits, I could see the look of anticipation on his face. He motioned me to come closer, "Karen, I had a visitor last night, and he told me something about Kathy."

"Really, Dad? Who was that?"

He lowered his voice as if it was a secret, and the expression on his face became very serious. "It was the old police chief of Franklin, and before I died he wanted me to know who killed Kathy. He said it was the man who has been a major suspect all along." He proceeded to tell me the man's name, and sure enough, it was the man who had been a prime suspect all these years, and it wasn't the man who rented the apartment upstairs. After he told me his secret, he seemed relieved, closed his eyes, and fell asleep.

As he slept, I wondered why the retired police chief waited until my dad was dying to give him that information. Why not before?

Why, if he was so sure of who it was, did they not do anything about it in the past? Was he trying to relieve some guilt that he had been carrying all these years? Was he looking to clear his conscience, thinking that the failure to make an arrest for Kathy's murder would be easier to digest? The murder was in 1971 and reopened in 1983. Now it was 1992 and still no one had been charged for this crime. My dad would never see that day. I touched his hand and told him I would see him later. "Sleep well, Dad. I love you."

On the drive home, I thought about the information my dad had given me. It brought up memories of the past and the reminder that something wasn't right with this investigation. I wasn't the only one who felt that way in my family. My family, including my dad, had felt for some time now that things didn't seem to add up with Kathy's case. Our suspicion really surfaced during the reopening of Kathy's murder in 1983.

As time passed by, the family began to question the investigation. We reviewed some of the events of 1971, and felt that there may have been errors. We were suspicious enough that we hesitated to speak with some who had been involved in the initial investigation. Whom could we trust if information came our way? In 1983, I was told by a detective that mistakes were made by those investigating the case in 1971. He explained that they did the best they could with what they had to work with. But it was more than that; something didn't add up.

How could we prove it? None of us knew whom to trust, but we did know that something hadn't come out, and had been shoved to the bottom of the compost pile in hopes that it would never be found.

Somehow, someway, someone interfered with the investigation of Kathy's death. Her murder would never be solved until someone was willing to expose the corruption. Ten years had gone by since the reactivation. They were "that close" to bringing someone in, but nothing happened. Absolutely nothing.

Perhaps strength doesn't reside in having
never been broken...but in the courage
required to grow strong in the broken places.

RUTHIE DEAN
*

CHAPTER THIRTY

The day finally came when the phone rang, and I was told to come to the Veterans Home. They said my father wasn't doing well. Ann, Janet, and I spent the whole day there and stayed with him into the night. We were all exhausted from the long days and from the emotional strain of watching him slip away.

The next day, the three of us were back in my dad's room realizing that his time to leave this world, and us, was near. I recognized some of the visible signs the body produces when a person has little time left. We wanted to make sure that someone was with him right to the end; we didn't want him to die alone. I think our concern came from knowing Kathy didn't have any of us with her when she faced death's door. The thought of her being alone without a loved one nearby left a mark on all our hearts, and it wasn't something we wanted for Dad.

During the day, I was able to have some time with my dad alone. As I was standing next to his bed, he raised his arms up and brought his hands together, fingers interlocked as though he wanted to pray.

My dad was never a religious man. I don't remember him going to church with us, and it wasn't like him to pray openly. Seeing his hands come together to pray surprised me.

Mike and I talked to him off and on over the years about God. He was bitter about a number of things in his life; some were self-inflicted but some were with just cause. One night he told me, "God could never forgive me for what I've done in my life, what I did during the war," and he began to cry. I told him that even though war is ugly, sometimes it's necessary. Even in the Bible there were times God sent His people out to war.

"God can forgive you, Dad. He sent His Son so that we could have forgiveness for the things we've done. He knows about all of them, and He still loves you."

He just sat there and cried. Some people feel that they don't need forgiveness no matter what they've done, but that wasn't the case with my dad. He knew he needed forgiveness for things he had done, but he couldn't believe that God could be merciful enough to actually do it. He had been given a way to know for sure that he was going to heaven, but he never really accepted the truth we gave him.

Friends of ours had spoken to him also, but sadly, sometimes knowing and understanding doesn't always end in acceptance. Years earlier, he prayed with Mike and me. After he prayed, he made the following statement: "Now maybe my luck will change." My heart sank. I knew my dad. He was hoping that since he had prayed, his chances of winning the lottery had just increased. Seeing him raise his hands in prayer at the end of his life was unexpected. I asked him,

"Dad, are you trying to pray?" No response, yet his arms stayed up and his fingers stayed interlocked. I began to quote Scripture to him about trusting in Christ for his eternal life. "Dad, all of us come short of God's glory. *For all have sinned, and come short of the glory of God*" (Romans 3:23). Then I quoted Romans 6:23, "*For the wages of sin is death; but the gift of God is eternal life through Jesus Christ our Lord,*" and Romans 10:13, "*For whosoever shall call upon the name of the Lord shall be saved.*"

I spoke gently and said, "Dad, you can have peace about your eternity; you know the way. *Jesus saith unto him, "I am the way, the truth, and the life: no man cometh unto the Father, but by me*" (John 14:6). I leaned closer and whispered, "All you have to do, Dad, is believe, believe in your heart." With that, he slowly and deliberately nodded in acknowledgment and then put his hands by his sides once again. That was the last movement I saw him make except for the shallow, labored breaths he took. I gave him a kiss, "Rest now, Dad. Today you will be in heaven with Kathy. This is what you've been waiting for."

I closed my eyes and thanked the Lord, "I will never forget this, God. Thank you for your love and mercy."

Shortly after that, Ann and Janet came into the room, and we stayed close by his side. We passed the time by trying to make small talk, knowing that soon we would see our dad passing from this life to the next. I would miss him, but I knew that where he was going would be better than anything he could experience here.

His pain would be gone, but most importantly, his sorrow would be lifted. He would not have to shed any more tears for the son who died before him or for the little girl who was so brutally murdered and taken from him way before her time. The guilt of not being there to protect her when she needed him most would no longer consume him.

Ann and Janet decided to take a quick trip to get some coffee. They had just left the room and were nearly out the main door when my dad began to breathe in an abnormal pattern. I knew this was a sign that he was very close to death. I ran down the hallway and yelled for Ann and Janet to come back. We stood close by his bed, held his hands, and rubbed his arms as we watched him labor for every breath. We wanted him to know that we were with him, and we weren't going to leave his side. One by one we told him it was okay to go. There was no holding back the tears for any of us.

All of a sudden his breathing stopped and we thought he was gone, but with a gasp he took another breath. It seemed as though this went on forever, until he finally stopped breathing altogether, and we knew it was done. He had finally gone on to heaven to meet those who had gone on before him. We sobbed, said goodbye, and held one another until we were ready to walk out of the room and let someone know he had passed away.

I had never seen someone go from life to death before. I had only seen them after they had already died. That's how it was with Kathy and with Richard. Watching Dad go from life to death made a great impact on me. When his last breath was taken and I knew it was over, I looked at him and for the first time in my life I realized that the body is just a shell, that it was the blood that sustained his life, and without the blood there is no life. Immediately I thought about the words in an old hymn: "What can wash away my sin? Nothing but the blood of

Jesus. What can make me whole again? Nothing but the blood of Jesus" (words and music by Robert Lowry). *And almost all things by the law purged with blood; and without shedding of blood is no remission* (Hebrews 9:22).

Oh yes, the blood gives us life, and Christ's blood gives us eternal life. I knew in an instant that Dad wasn't there, that his soul had gone on, that without the blood pumping through his body there was no life. It reinforced to me that the shed blood of Jesus Christ was essential for eternal life. We held hands and hugged one another in the hallway. Once our emotions were in control, we left to give my mom the news that Dad had died.

I look up to the sky and talk to you. What I wouldn't give to hear you talk back. I miss your voice, I miss your laughter, I miss everything about you.

UNKNOWN
*

CHAPTER THIRTY-ONE

It was going to be hard to tell Mom that Dad had passed away. Watching her live without the man she depended on all these years would be even harder. Richard's death and Kathy's murder put such a strain on their relationship, but I believe they never stopped loving each other.

We all went to my mom's apartment to give her the news. As we walked in, the look on our faces told her why we were there. One of the first things Mom asked was whether or not I thought he was in heaven. I explained to her what had happened just hours before he died. She knew my dad was a man without faith, but I assured her that he had accepted Christ. Many people realize their need for a Savior just before they die, and my dad was one of them.

"There is no doubt in my mind, Mom, that he understood and had peace about where he was going when death finally made its way to him. Don't worry. He's in a place where there is no more pain or tears. The burdens of this world are lifted."

Though his death brought her sorrow, I could see in her eyes that she was comforted in knowing that he was at peace.

Even now, I continue to be thankful that someone who had no faith in God came to know Him in a personal way at the end of his life. There are some who are weary of deathbed confessions. I say praise God that even in the very last moments of a person's life, one can know Christ's love and forgiveness.

We found out from the caretaker of the cemetery where Kathy had been buried that there wasn't enough room to have my dad placed in the ground beside her if it was a regular burial. But if he was to be cremated, there was enough room. So the decision was made that he would lie next to his daughter. And even though I knew that neither of their souls would be in that place, I felt in some way that he finally was able to watch over her and protect her as he wished he could have done that night she was taken from him so long ago.

I took three items from my dad's apartment. I took a padded box and frame I had made him years before as a Christmas gift. That year, Mike and I had very little money and couldn't afford to buy store-bought gifts. The frame held a picture of me, Mike, and the girls so he would be reminded of how much we loved him. I had filled the padded box with his favorite candy; he loved sweets. I also took a photo album that said Grandpa on the front and filled it with photos of his grand-daughters from various years. He cherished that album. As I looked at the items I removed from his apartment, a memory was stirred. I could see him tearing away the paper from the gifts that were carefully made for him. I was worried about how he might feel about the presents he was getting because they didn't come from a store. As he opened them, his face lit up. "You made this?" he said with a look of disbelief.

"Yes, Dad. Why do you look so surprised?"

He smiled at me. "It's very nice; I really like it."

Months later I went into his room and didn't see the frame or box on his bureau, and I asked him what he had done with it. He told me that he kept it in his bureau drawer because he didn't want it to get dirty. That was very sweet of him; it emphasized to me how much he cherished it.

Mike felt the loss of my dad greatly. Dad was known to chase a boy out of our house on a number of occasions, but Mike was not one of them. He was one of the few boys my dad actually liked. He enjoyed conversation with Mike, and Mike could make him laugh. Those two things were not easy to do when it came to my dad.

Joscelyn, Melissa, and Nicole would miss their pepé; they had a special bond with him. He wasn't one to give out a lot of hugs and kisses, but they always knew he loved them. It was the little things he did that ensured them of a love that was hard for him to express. I often wondered if he was afraid of getting too close, afraid of loving a child too deeply in case one day she would be snatched from him. He may have seemed crusty and hard to others, but to my girls, his heart was always tender.

Every rainbow begins with rain.

UNKNOWN
*

CHAPTER THIRTY-TWO

The next five years were filled with raising children, running a home, and being involved with church. It was a time without tragedy, and I welcomed it like the warmth of spring after a harsh winter. There were no more deaths to face, and I hadn't heard much about Kathy's case since Dad had died in 1992. Kathy's case had once again been put on a shelf, pushed to the back, and forgotten by everyone except for her family.

Mike and I and the girls fell into the routines of everyday life. We stayed involved in the girls' lives, and things finally seemed normal. The days were filled with school, piano lessons, basketball, volleyball, and other activities they were involved in. We were very active in the church we attended, and that filled any space that was left in our lives.

We took family vacations—mostly day trips to the lakes, ocean, or mountains. Money was usually tight, so we tried to plan things that would create longtime memories but were inexpensive. We went strawberry picking and made it a family event. We took trips to the ocean in the summer. The long ride helped to build the excitement of what was to come. Sometimes I leaned my head against the window and felt the warmth of the sun on my face. It brought therapy to a mom exhausted by three little girls.

I loved feeling the glorious rays of the sun, the sand between my toes, and taking in the smell of the ocean air with its gentle breezes. I watched the girls laugh as they built sandcastles with Mike and played in the water; and watched them run as the waves tried to capture them in a game of tag. The perfect ending was a stop at the clam shack on the way home for fried clams and ice cream. Traces of the sand brought home from tiny feet would be found in the car for weeks. It came with the territory and created memories to be placed in a treasure chest full of them.

Apple picking in the fall was a tradition. It included the enjoyment of biting into a caramel apple followed by a country ride on the back roads of New Hampshire. Fall was our favorite time of the year; and even though there were times when we had to share one of those caramel apples because money was scarce, we didn't care. Seeing the fall colors splashed across the canvas of an old New England road has always been one of my favorite things.

Over the years I have learned that my heart can contain great pain and sorrow, but it can also contain love and joy if I allow them in. My goal was to continue to fill my heart with as many treasured memories as I could, and in doing so, the pain occupied less space.

CHAPTER THIRTY-THREE

In June 1997, Mike's boss talked to him about being in charge of a project the company was taking on. It involved building a new plant and leading the startup of production. This would entail deciding what state it would be in, purchasing land, designing and building the new facility, and getting it up and running. He was long overdue for a change in his job and was excited about this new opportunity.

When he told Nicole and me of the job opportunity, he also mentioned that he was going to pray about specifics to help him decide whether or not to take this job. He decided on a salary and the details of a moving package.

"If they don't offer me what I have in mind, it'll show me that the door to this job is closed," he said. Nicole and I sat there thinking that this move was probably not going to happen.

The following evening he came home and said he had something to tell me. "Karen, they offered me a package to take this job. Without telling them any of the details, they made an offer with the exact salary and moving package I prayed about." We both were amazed and felt that it was a door that the Lord had opened for us.

We would be leaving New Hampshire and our friends and family. Nicole would be leaving a school she had gone to since first grade. It would be tough on her, but I knew this opportunity was a good one. He would have a change in his job, and we would eventually have a chance to move back to New Hampshire in the future if we wanted. I talked to Nicole about the sacrifices her dad had made for us over the years and how he had worked very hard to provide everything we had. The least we could do was see him through this and be willing to sacrifice for him.

Nicole was going to be a sophomore in high school, and we made a pact with her that if she wanted to go back to New Hampshire for her senior year and graduate with the kids she grew up with, we would work it out. She didn't like that we were moving, but I encouraged her to make the best of it. Of course, we hoped she would adjust and want to stay in California to finish her senior year.

For some time I hadn't been feeling well. I had numbness in my lips, arms, and legs accompanied by nausea and tiredness. There were times when I needed to lie down. I would fall asleep for five minutes or so and then wake up feeling fine. My family practitioner, whom I had learned to love over the years, wanted me to see a neurologist. She was a rare breed in her profession, and the thought of trying to find a new doctor in California was discouraging. She had known me for years and tenderly cared for my family. All my daughters had gone to her since they were little girls; she always made them feel comfortable.

I would schedule an appointment in October, and she immediately knew it was my season for bronchitis and sinus infections. Whenever I went to her office, she would inquire about the family and how Mike's golf game was going. I had a feeling I would never find another doctor like her.

I stopped in to see my mom at her apartment. She hadn't been calling me for some reason, so I wanted to check up on her. I also needed to tell her about Mike and the position he had taken in California. I walked in and she was sitting in her usual chair, looking at magazines.

"Hi, Mom, how are you doing?"

"I'm fine," she said.

We chatted about the girls and how they were doing in school, and then I broke the news. "Mike is taking a new job that was offered to him, and we are moving to California."

I explained all the circumstances, trying to be sympathetic. Although Joscelyn was away at college, her other two grandchildren, Melissa and Nicole, would be coming with us and that would be difficult for her. Mom sat there and didn't say much of anything. I did most of the talking. I really loved my mom and had learned to deal with her personality over the years. I kept in mind the painful memories she had to live with and learned to let things go.

"I don't know how long we'll be in California, Mom, but Janet will still be here to help you and watch out for you. Who knows? We could be back in New Hampshire within a few years." I explained to her how much stress Mike had been under with his job, and how he looked forward to this new challenge. She just sat there, not wanting to participate in any of the conversation.

Then I talked to her about how I had not been feeling well and the doctor wanted me to have some tests done before I moved. "She wants me to see a neurologist for some reason. I wasn't going to go, but someone from the doctor's office called and said they had already made an appointment for me. I told her I wasn't planning on going to a neurologist, and she said that the doctor felt it was important."

She continued to sit there listening, never asking any questions. I told her I would let her know when I heard something. "Things are going to be crazy, Mom. We need to get things in order for the move. Movers will be coming, and then I need to have these medical tests done. I will make sure we all come over to see you to say goodbye."

I got up to leave, gave her a kiss and hug, and said goodbye. I waved to her as I went out the door and never thought it was going to be the last day I would see her. My family would soon face another unexpected death, which would leave a very deep wound.

CHAPTER THIRTY-FOUR

On July 17, 1997, my phone rang, and I heard Janet's voice on the other end. I could sense at once that she had bad news. Her voice was trembling as she said, "Mom died. She committed suicide last night in her apartment." I could hear her crying.

"What?" I said in disbelief. I put the phone to my chest, looked up with pleading eyes, and prayed, "Oh, God, help me." In an instant I felt utterly exhausted, not from any physical activity, but from life itself. I got back on the phone, and through my tears I asked Janet to tell me what happened.

Late the night before, Mom called her social worker several times but no one answered. Was Mom hoping that her message might prompt a phone call that would stop her? She left a message saying that she wasn't going to be around for a while because she was going on a trip, and she wanted to say goodbye.

The next morning, her social worker went to her apartment to check on her because of the messages left on the answering machine the night before. She entered her apartment and found Mom's lifeless body with a note explaining why she had taken her own life.

The police and ambulance were called, and Janet was notified. When the police officer talked to Janet, he told her that it looked like suicide. They found a note, but still had to determine cause of death. Once that was done, the note would be turned over to the family.

Janet finished filling in the details, and we were both silent for a moment. I was stunned. "I can't believe she killed herself. I was with her the other day and she seemed fine. She didn't say or do anything that indicated she was contemplating suicide. I'm shocked. How could she do this?"

Janet sighed heavily and replied, "I was supposed to go over there this morning. What if I walked into her apartment and found her? What if I had the boys with me? That would have been horrible. She knew I was coming; didn't she think about that?" With sadness in our voices, we said our goodbyes and planned to meet the next day.

I sat on the edge of my bed, slowly lowered my head to my pillow, and began to weep. I cried until I was sick and had to run to the bathroom. I stayed on the floor of the bathroom until I felt strong enough to get up and then called Mike at work to tell him the news and ask him to come home. I couldn't wait for him to hold me.

The coroner verified that my mother had taken prescription medications to end her life. This wasn't the first time she attempted to end her life; the difference was that this time she succeeded. Even before Kathy's murder, she struggled to appreciate what was really valuable and important. Then she experienced one of the most disheartening things a parent could ever go through—her child was unexpectedly and violently ripped from her, snatched from her loving arms, never to be held again.

Not only did she lose her youngest child, but she also endured having her son pass away before her. She lost a husband whom she depended on, and although their relationship was strained, she missed his companionship.

She was tired of life; there was no doubt of that. Her journey was finished, but ours would go on to bear this additional tragedy. How was I going to explain this to the girls? They loved her. It would be hard for them to understand why they weren't enough of a reason for her to keep on living. I needed to make sure they understood that what she did had nothing to do with them. She took her life because she was distraught and in pain, but I wished she could have realized all that she had to live for.

I prayed over the years that God would never let me get to the point of taking my own life. Understanding the destruction it would leave behind convinced me it could never be a way out. How could I let my family think that I would choose death over life with them?

When I felt like giving up, I quickly tried to fill my mind with a list of what was most precious to me, my list of thankfulness. Then I realized life was better than death, because with death came departure from those I cherish and love. Plus, the hurt and sorrow I would leave behind from taking my own life would be like a flooded river rushing recklessly through a town, destroying everything in its path.

We watched out for my mom and helped her when she needed it. Roger sent money to help her financially. Ann made sure she stayed in touch and visited whenever she was in town. Because Janet and I lived the closest to her, we were in and out of her apartment all the time. We made sure she had contact with her grandchildren, spent time with her, and took her to places she needed to go.

As far as I could tell, she was doing well. She kept the weight on that she had gained while living with us, and she made some close friendships with people who lived in her apartment complex. Life was back to the way it should be. She portrayed one who was enjoying life and was back to her old activities, including Bingo. She played that game for as long as I can remember.

Even with the shock of my mother's death, I still had to proceed with the tests the doctor had arranged for me. In the midst of all this, I had movers coming to the house to pack our things for our move to California. Mom knew when we would be moving. Did she plan her suicide to make sure that I would still be in town? The note she left behind was disturbing. She knew that this note would be the final words she left for others to remember her by. I had a sea of emotions running through me—sympathy for her, sadness for my loss, and anger with her for causing such hurt to me and to the rest of my family.

I know life was hard for her, and I sympathized with her because of that. As children, it wasn't easy for us either; there were many burdens to bear. For Janet and me it was especially difficult because we were the ones who dealt with her during our own traumatic times. But no matter how hard things got, we loved her very much.

Over the years, I wished that life was easier for her and my dad. I wanted peace and happiness for her. Janet and I both did whatever we could to ease her path in life, but life had taken its toll, and I guess she saw no other way out.

I battled with the fact that she chose death over life. I knew that by doing so she was going to miss out on so much. She wouldn't see her grandchildren grow up or be a part of their lives. She would never see them perform in another school program, celebrate a graduation, or watch them walk the aisle on their wedding day. She would never know the blessing of having great-grandchildren. There would be many wonderful events she would miss out on because she chose not to be here for the future.

I understood that someone ready to commit suicide was not usually thinking logically, so I tried not to be angry with her. What was the sense in being angry with someone who was no longer living? It didn't make the sadness go away. I also understood that sometimes life could be unbearable. Some people would do anything for relief. They grasp at whatever will ease or end their anguish. Still, it seemed like such a selfish choice. Did Mom not comprehend the aftermath of her decision? I wished she could see how much more life had to offer her. God knew, Mom. He knew the darkness you carried.

I looked to God for answers. "Tell me why, God? Why did she have to do that? Didn't she realize what it would do to us? How it might hurt us?" As children and young adults, we also had been through so much. Now we had another tragedy to put into the chest that was already full.

"God, help me. Please help me not to be angry or bitter. Help me to understand the reason why she made such a choice."

A few days later, we met at Mom's apartment to begin going through her things and to discuss her funeral arrangements. When I got to the apartment, they were all sitting in the living room. I told Janet that I wanted to read the note, and she began to cry.

"What's the matter?" I asked.

Janet just looked at me. I turned toward Ann, and she also had tears in her eyes. Roger just sat there staring at me.

"Give me the note. I want to read it," I said. "What is going on, and why don't you want me to read it? Janet, just give me the note."

She reluctantly handed me the note. As I read, I began to sob. For some reason Mom felt that there were people out to get her and hurt her. You could tell she was in a confused state of mind, and her handwriting showed that the pills had already taken affect. I understood why Janet wanted to keep it from me, but I wasn't a little girl anymore, and I needed to know.

Mom mentioned how much she missed and wanted to be with Dad, Richard, and Kathy. She expressed that whoever hurt Kathy was going to pay for what they had done, and somehow she would make sure of that. She left instructions on how she wanted to be buried and what to do with her things. She had a small bird and wanted to make sure it was cared for. She wanted the social worker to know she was sorry for what she was going to do, and also apologized to some of her neighbors she had gotten close to.

To Ann, Janet, and Roger she expressed her apologies for taking her life. Not once was I mentioned in the suicide note. My heart was terribly broken, and I couldn't imagine what she was thinking to do such a thing. Her thought process was beyond my understanding and affected me for a long time. I would live the rest of my life knowing that she was angry with me for some reason.

So many things were running through my mind. Did she leave a note like that because she felt I had thrown her out when I suggested she get a place of her own? It was so long ago, and I couldn't imagine that she was still upset about that. Was it because I had just told her that Mike and I were moving, and she wouldn't see the girls like she used to? Those were the only things I could think of that would upset her. All I could think was that she was angry with me because we were moving. She knew the date we would be leaving, and she made sure that she ended her life before I was gone. She must have known that it would break my heart when I found out that she had taken her own life. Reading the note she left behind was like pouring salt on an open wound. The sting from it was almost unbearable.

I knew in my heart that it was going to be important to forgive her. It would be crucial for stability in my life and in keeping my heart tender. But when I read the suicide note, it was like a hot poker piercing my heart; it was painful, and I was crushed. As I thought about what she wrote, the words Christ spoke as he hung on the cross came to mind. "Then, said Jesus, *Father, forgive them; for they know not what they do*" (Luke 23:34). I prayed and asked God to help me remember all that he had forgiven me for. God had given His Son so that I might have eternal life, and I needed to remember that I had not yet endured what Christ did on the cross. If Christ could do that for me and for a world that was so undeserving, I had to find peace in my heart about what she had done. If I could keep that in mind in the days and months ahead, I knew I would be okay.

As the verse continued to float around in my head, I whispered, "I love you, Mom."

She didn't want a viewing at a funeral home, just a ceremony at the cemetery. Like my father, Mom wanted to be cremated and placed on the other side of Kathy's grave. One on each side, they would lie next to her; it was a fitting place for them to be. But I knew their final destination was not in the ground, but in heaven, a glorious place that had been prepared for them. They were in a place of no more tears and no more sorrow. Neither of them had to be sad anymore, and that was comforting to me.

I loved my mom and though her death was painful, I was thankful that she didn't have to suffer any longer. She would no longer suffer physically or mentally. She finally had found a place of peace and joy. No longer would she have the thoughts that tormented her over the years. I spent so much time in prayer asking God to continually give me a heart of tenderness and understanding about what she had done. I did not want my heart to be filled with anger or bitterness.

My health spiraled. I was exhausted and emotionally drained. I couldn't eat and was constantly in the bathroom getting sick. The moving company was coming to pack us for the move to California. Our dog had to be placed with its breeder because we couldn't find a place to rent in the area that would accept dogs. I still had medical tests to be done. And I was still trying to cope with the overwhelming reality of my mom's death. I felt physically sick all day long.

My first scheduled test was the MRI, which proved that there was nothing wrong with my brain, although I knew some who would argue that point. I was thankful not to be facing brain surgery. Next came the EEG to find out if I was having seizures. I still considered this a waste of time, but the neurologist thought it was important for me to have it done before I left for California.

Since our house was packed for the move, we stayed with our friends, Rich and Pat. They were such a blessing to us during this time. Pat was my best friend, a kindred spirit, someone I could talk to about all that I was going through. I was going to miss her; friends like that don't come around every day. Both Rich and Pat were godly people and really loved the Lord and I treasured their spiritual guidance in my life. Opening their home to brothers and sisters in Christ was a common occurrence. They were very generous with all the Lord had given them. I was not looking forward to leaving such dear friends.

The medical tests brought added stress beyond what I felt I could handle. We were moving to a new location, but all that had happened would follow me. I wished I could leave all the sadness behind and move forward. I wanted to box up the hurts of Kathy's murder, Richard's death, watching my dad slowly succumb to cancer, and Mom's recent decision to take her own life. If I could take it all—the sadness, the hurt—and put it in a box, lock it, and throw away the key, I would. I was tired, so very tired.

The EEG required being sleep deprived, so I had to stay up most of the night. Pat tried to stay up with me as long as she could but finally, with heavy eyes, she said, "I have to go to bed. I can't stay up any longer. I'm old."

"Oh sure, what kind of friend are you?" I joked. "You can't even stay up with me all night." We laughed, and off she went to bed. It was a struggle to stay awake, but I managed to get through the night, got dressed in the morning, and Mike took me in for the test.

As the technician placed the goop on my head and attached all the necessary wires, I thought of telling him it was a waste of time to look for any brain activity because at this point I was pretty sure there was none. My brain felt empty and so did my heart.

I considered asking, "Hey, could you put those on my heart because I think it stopped beating." I was emotionally and physically exhausted and really just wanted to sleep. When the test was finished, Mike came back and picked me up, and I finally went to bed. I felt like saying, "I'm going to sleep, and don't ever wake me up."

The following day was busy, we still had things to do before our move. When we returned to the house that evening, Pat told me that the doctor had called. It was around midnight, so I thought I would call her the following day or maybe when I got to California. But Pat said the doctor wanted me to call her at her home and it didn't matter what time it was. I looked at Pat. "I'm sure it's just to tell me everything is fine. Maybe I need some other test done when I get to California." Pat reiterated what the doctor said. "She told me it was very important that you call before you leave, and it didn't matter what time it was."

I made the phone call and told my neurologist that I was sorry it was so late but I had just gotten home. "Karen, I'm so sorry about your mom. I heard she passed away last week." My mom had also been a patient of hers years ago, so she knew her and about Kathy's murder, and how difficult my mom's life was because of it. "Thank you," I said. "She didn't have the emotional strength to go on. She missed those who went on before her—Kathy, my brother, and also my dad. She never was able to cope with the loss of Kathy. Her life was never the same after that. None of our lives were ever the same."

"Well, I don't know that I could go on if I lost one of my children like that either," she said. She told me again she was sorry for the loss of my mother and then told me she had gotten the results from my EEG. "Your results came in, and I wanted to speak with you before you left for California."

"Okay," I said, wondering what she possibly could tell me. "The test revealed that you're having partial seizures. Karen, you need to be on medication to control them. I would get you started, but since you're leaving for California, it would be better if you found a neurologist out there and worked with him to regulate the seizures."

I was shocked. There is no way the test could be accurate. "Are you sure?"

I associated epilepsy with blackouts, and I had never had any, so I thought the test had to be wrong. She explained to me the difference between grand mal and partial seizures. As she was explaining it, I recalled a girl I knew in grade school who had grand mal seizures. I remembered a time when we were all out for recess. She fell in the schoolyard and blacked out. It was awful to watch. As children, we thought it was because something was wrong with her mentally.

Even though I had been feeling pretty sick at times, throwing up for no reason, I was convinced it had to be something else causing it. "Wouldn't anyone who is sleep deprived and going through a lot of stress show abnormal brain waves?" I asked her.

"No," she said. "The man who did your test is one of the best in the state, and I have no doubt that it is accurate. You cannot drive until you see a doctor in California and get on medication to make sure the seizures are regulated. It is state law that I notify the Motor Vehicle Department about your results; your license will be revoked until they know you are seizure free. Every state has different requirements," she informed me.

"But I've never had a blackout, and they must be so subtle that no one would ever know I was having them."

She explained, "Any time a person with seizures is not on medication, they can have a grand mal if a burst of electricity travels from the left side of the brain to the right. It can cause a blackout. This is serious, Karen."

To emphasize her point, she gave me information on a true case that had happened not long ago. "There was a person in California who had these same types of seizures and was told not to drive until they got on medication. He never had a blackout either. He ignored his doctor and drove anyway. He had his first blackout going over the Golden Gate Bridge in San Francisco and killed two people."

Okay, I thought. She made her point with that story.

"As soon as you get out to California, find a neurologist. He will start you on medication and regulate the seizures. You'll be amazed at how much better you'll feel. I'm sorry again about your mom and about this news, but now we know why you haven't been feeling good for so long."

All I could say was, "Thank you." In shock, I sat down by the bay window and tried to process what the doctor had just told me. God, are You there? I need You.

I walked into the living room where Mike, Pat, and Rich were talking, and stood at the top of the stairs. Tearfully, I stood there looking at them. I was numb.

"What's the matter? What did she say?" Mike asked.

With an expression of disbelief I said, "She said I have epilepsy."

Mike looked as surprised as I did. "What? Are you sure that's what she said?"

I explained the test results to him. Just as I had, he questioned the accuracy of the test. I told him that the man who did the test was one of the best in the state and that the neurologist had no doubt that the results were accurate. Pat came over and gave me a big hug. I hadn't even gotten a grip on my mom's death yet and now this. I wasn't sure I believed what I had just been told. Moving to another state would be hard enough, never mind finding a specialist right away. The thought of not being able to drive was very troubling. Whew, my plate was definitely full, and I couldn't quite digest it all.

That night when everyone else was sleeping, I lay in bed just staring at the ceiling. This is a joke, right, God? You can't be serious. Do You really think that I can handle all of this?

I knew God's Word told me He would never leave me nor forsake me, but at that moment I felt alone.

CHAPTER THIRTY-FIVE

Saying goodbye to dear friends in New Hampshire was a difficult thing to do. I had mixed feelings about leaving the area. I was sad to leave those I loved and the things that were familiar. Not having friends around would make getting through the emotional process more difficult.

During this trying time, I turned to the Scriptures for guidance. I went to the book of Job. He was a man who had it all, and in the blink of an eye, everything he had and the people he cherished were taken from him. And yet his love for God remained, and in the end God blessed him beyond anyone's imagination. This scripture always showed me that there were those who had gone through more than I had, and it put things in perspective. Contemplating Christ's death and Job's life made me thankful for what I had.

Job suffered tremendously, but God never let him go; and at the end of all his suffering, God replaced all that he had lost and more. He restored Job and gave him peace and happiness again. This I clung to during the trials in my life. I tried to remember that after the storm, peace would come again. I claimed Isaiah 43:2 as my life verse: When thou passest through the waters, I will be with thee; and through the rivers, they shall not overflow thee: when thou walkest through the fire, thou shalt not be burned; neither shall the flame kindle upon thee.

The next scriptures I went to were Psalms and Proverbs. It was easy reading, and the treasures in those two books were phenomenal. I reminded myself of what my Savior did for me, remembering the tremendous suffering He endured and His willingness to go to the cross. He did it all because He loved me. I could not comprehend such amazing love.

There were times in my life that the people I loved helped me climb some of the mountains, but only God brought me to the top. This was one of those times. I was climbing the mountain and totally exhausted, trying to do too much on my own. I was ready for God to carry me the rest of the way. God, it's You and me; I'm waiting. Don't let me go; I'm afraid.

As I adjusted to life in California, I learned to depend on others to drive me around. It was exasperating looking for new doctors; my patience was tested. While trying to cope with my mother's death, God's Word kept it all in perspective. I clung to my Bible as if it were an old tattered and torn security blanket, not wanting to let it go for fear that it might be misplaced or never found again.

I faced each day like a spectator at a football game. I was not actually involved in the game, just watching from the sidelines. I smiled when I was supposed to smile, responded when I was supposed to respond, and did the daily activities that were expected of me. I tried to stay focused; but throughout the day, I felt as though I was drifting deeper into my own thoughts.

Mike was working on a new building and starting up production for his company, so he was able to work at home for months. I definitely put it on my list of things to be thankful for—my faithful list that would appear during tough times. It was hard to concentrate. I would start making the list, but my mind would wander and I'd have to start over again. That happened a lot; when I read my Bible, I found myself reading the same thing over and over. When I prayed, my thoughts would drift. It was a good thing my relationship with God wasn't based upon how well I concentrated or how much I accomplished in my Bible reading and prayer life.

When we moved to California, Joscelyn was in college, and I missed her. I cherished her support through cards and letters and couldn't wait until she came home again. Melissa and Nicole were in California with us, and I didn't know what I would do without them. I had to depend on Melissa and Mike to drive me to and from stores, doctor appointments, and anywhere else I needed or wanted to go. Melissa had never driven on busy freeways before, and it was very stressful for her and for me. She drove her sister to school, drove herself to classes, and then picked up Nicole from school.

Melissa was a good driver, but it didn't matter. I was always nervous when she drove and thought for sure we were going to die on the freeway. When she drove I made noises or would say "Watch out," and cause her to be even more nervous. "Mom, you're going to make me get in an accident if you don't quit it," she would say. I don't know how many times I had to bite my tongue and just pray.

One night I saved us from landing in a canal. The road curved ahead, but it was dark and hard to see. If we didn't make the turn, we were going to end up in one of the irrigation canals. I grabbed the wheel to turn it. "What are you doing?" she yelled. "I'm just saving our lives, thank you very much," I yelled back. The rest of the ride home was a little tense. She took on a lot of responsibility, and I was truly thankful. I don't know what I would have done without her. She became my best friend that year.

Nicole had a tough year adjusting to a new school; she played volleyball and basketball. She tried her hand at softball, which was a game she had never played before. I worried about her and hoped that she would adjust. I knew from experience that at her age, the world and everyone in it could seem to be against you, and there was a danger of becoming too self-absorbed. I prayed that the Lord would show her what was important in life.

Watching her play sports was a gift for me; it helped focus my energy on other things. Mike and I enjoyed going to her games and watching her excel to new levels. She took driver's education and got her license. We limited her driving; most of it consisted of going to and from school. One day she came home and told us she needed her own car, and my reply was, "When you get a job and can pay for your own car, then you can have a car. Until then, be thankful that you have any car at all to drive." Her driving record was good except for the day she pulled into the garage, stepped on the gas instead of the brake, and literally drove into the wall that connected the garage to the house. All I can say is, good thing for insurance because there was a lot of damage done to the house and to the car. The look on her face was priceless, and even though it wasn't funny at the time, it certainly was later.

Whenever a new year began, I took the previous year's calendar and transferred birthdays and anniversaries to the new calendar. We moved to California in July of 1997, the same month my mom died and I was diagnosed with seizures. It was now January 1, 1998, and I sat down to the yearly task of making sure important events and dates were posted on the calendar for the new year.

As I went from month to month, I relived the previous year. I read through the events surrounding my mom's death and all that had happened during the year. It was overwhelming, and I started to cry uncontrollably. "I should be a nut case," I said out loud. I knew that my faith was the only reason I wasn't in some institution. I clung to God's promise in 2 Timothy 1:7: "For God hath not given us the Spirit of fear; but of power, and of love, and of a sound mind." Oh, how I thanked Him for not changing. He was always the same. Where else in life could I find such stability?

Melissa was engaged, and I focused on planning her December wedding. Though we lived in California, the wedding would be held in New Hampshire. The planning was stressful, but it was a good stress. We were on a budget, so I tried to make whatever I could to keep the cost down. Melissa wanted her wedding to be simple but elegant. That phrase became a joke to Mike because he heard it so many times. I enjoyed the special time I had with Melissa—searching for wedding dresses, looking through bridal magazines, and making keepsakes. Since my wedding dress was never going to be used again, I cut it up and made ring bearer pillows and flower girl baskets out of the material. They would be unique lifelong keepsakes and would remind Melissa of a special day in her life and mine. It felt so good to be involved in something beautiful. My mind was occupied with making Melissa's wedding day special. God showed me that life could be good again, and the sadness began to slip away.

Melissa married Rich and Pat's son, Joshua, and moved to Florida. The wedding was beautiful. Her move was hard on Nicole and me; both of us had become so close to her during our time in California. When we got back from the wedding, Nicole and I stood in Melissa's bedroom filled with boxes ready to be shipped out. Together we began to cry and stood there hugging each other.

CHAPTER THIRTY-SIX

From 1997 to 2000, Mike was involved in building a new facility and getting production going. He completed the project on time and within budget. We built a house, and Nicole finished both her freshman and sophomore year. As promised, we were arranging her trip back to New Hampshire for her senior year so she could graduate with her childhood friends.

Mike developed a mysterious case of hives that the doctors could not figure out. Every day he worked through the swelling and discomfort and stayed faithful in church. I admired him for that. I wondered if I would stay faithful in the same situation, or if I would use the hives as an excuse not to go to church.

Joscelyn came home from college in 1998, worked, and took some classes. It was so good to have her around again. She was not only my daughter, she was my friend; and I looked forward to the time we spent together. I was glad she was able to go to college and spread her wings, but I was overjoyed that she was home again. She had become a beautiful young woman; so independent, so different from the little girl who used to send her little sister up to the food counter to ask for ketchup because she was too afraid. I was proud of the woman she had become and that she still had a love for the Lord.

Life in California fell into a steady rhythm, but I still had a lot of things to sort out spiritually and physically. I had to work not only through a medical condition, but also through hurt, anger, and forgiveness. Kathy's murder wreaked havoc on our already struggling family and stamped each of our lives with permanent sorrow. Forgiving Mom was the right thing to do, and I prayed for God to help me to forgive her as I had been forgiven.

Just when I thought I had gotten victory and forgiven her for taking her own life, something would happen and the old feelings would rise up like a river after a heavy spring rain. I begged the Lord, "Please, God, let me have a forgiving heart, one like Yours." I couldn't sort through all my feelings about her suicide and the note she left behind, but I did know that I loved her very much.

I looked to Him to show me how to forgive when I didn't understand a situation or when the pain was great. Christ forgave me, a sinner, and I didn't deserve it. He gave His life so that I might have eternal life. I wanted that kind of heart, not just with my mom, but with others too. That's when I began to pray for those who had been involved in the murder of my sister. I prayed not only for them to be caught and justice to be served but also for their souls and their eternal destination. They were not exempt from paying for the crime they committed while living on earth, but Christ could change their eternal destiny. I knew from the Bible what hell was going to be like, and I didn't wish for anyone to spend eternity there, even if I thought they deserved it. God gave all of us a way to avoid what we truly deserve; we all come short of His expectations, no matter how good we've been. It's a good thing it's not left up to me to decide who will go to heaven or hell. I wanted to see those involved in Kathy's murder punished for what they did, but I didn't wish any of them eternity in hell.

It was so long since we last heard anything about Kathy's case. My family had given up hope that anything would happen from the reopening. Mom and Dad were gone now, but we still desired justice for our sister. No one ever talked to us about why they had stopped working on the case.

I wondered when it was put back on the dusty shelves and stored away for a second time. Was this all we would ever get—reliving horrible memories, hoping that it might be solved, and then watching it slowly slip away?

On top of reliving Kathy's murder, we now believed that there had been interference in the original investigation, and that was very disturbing. We no longer felt this case involved just one person; there were others involved. Just as my mother knew in her heart that something terrible had happened the night Kathy disappeared, we knew as a family that something was terribly wrong with the way Kathy's investigation went in 1971.

We had only lived in the new house in California for a year when, in 2000, Mike's company wanted him back in New Hampshire to work in the Franklin facility. They wanted him back as soon as possible, so we started throwing stuff in boxes and suitcases, booking tickets to fly, and putting the house on the market. In two weeks the house sold, and we were on our way back to the state that held so many memories, both good and bad.

One great thing about the move was that we were going to be there for a good part of Nicole's senior year. I missed seeing her every day and watching her play sports. I wanted to be with her during her senior year, but I wasn't looking forward to moving back to New Hampshire just yet. I had a lot of skeletons to face. A lot had happened since I was a little girl growing up there. I always referred to New Hampshire as my home. I grew up there, was married there, and our children were born there. It's where I spent most of my life and had the deepest ties, not only to the past, but also to family and friends.

We looked for a house to buy but there wasn't much on the market, so Mike and I decided to build. As we waited for the house to be completed, we lived here and there and out of suitcases for over a year. We rented an apartment, stayed with friends, stayed in a lake house that was graciously offered to us, went back to an apartment, and back in with friends. It was a crazy year. The day the house was finished and we moved in was a blessing. It was a beautiful home on seven acres of land. We were so ready to settle down somewhere.

We planned another wedding for our youngest daughter, Nicole. She married Dan, the son of friends. Mike watched his baby girl get married, and I think it was harder on him than it was on me. When Josh and Melissa married, they moved to Florida. Dan and Nicole were staying in New Hampshire, and I counted that as a great blessing.

Joscelyn, our oldest, lived and worked in Colorado, and she loved it, except that she missed being near family. Eventually she moved to Connecticut to be closer to all of us. Some weekends she would travel to New Hampshire and stay with us. It wasn't uncommon that she would bring friends, and I loved the vitality they brought to our home.

Josh and Melissa eventually moved back to New Hampshire from Florida. I was so excited about the move. Melissa was pregnant, and Mike and I were going to enjoy the wonder of our first grandchild. It was so great to have all of our children nearby. What a joy it would be to love and spoil a child but not have to raise and discipline it.

When Josh and Melissa first moved back, they lived with us while they restored a home they had purchased. They came with a dog named Dakota, and this dog had some serious issues, but I won't get into that! I watched Melissa prepare for motherhood. She went into labor, and Mike and I were there with her and Josh. It was amazing to see our grandson born. I was glad I wasn't delivering. Josh was a little squeamish about cutting the cord, so Mike had the privilege of doing it. It was such a joyous day to greet Wyatt into our world.

Our grandson was in our home the first four months of his life. It was fun to hold him whenever I wanted, and with Melissa being a new mom, she cherished having the help. Mike looked forward to cuddling with Wyatt when he got home from work. The day Josh and Melissa moved out was tough, especially for Mike. They were only moving twenty minutes away, but it was still hard to see them go. At that point both Mike and I thought that maybe we should have had more children. I loved being a mom, and he loved being a dad.

I cherished all that the Lord had given us. The tragedies in my life had taught me never to take anything for granted; the lesson was engraved upon my heart. I knew from experience that the ones you loved could be taken away in a single moment.

We had a beautiful home with space for large family gatherings, and we took advantage of it. Mike had always wanted a great room in a house, but the joke in our new home was that I got a great kitchen instead. Having the girls, their husbands, and our grandchild nearby made our hearts full. I was especially thankful for the time of peace and rest that the Lord gave me; it was nourishing to my soul. But that was about to change.

CHAPTER THIRTY-SEVEN

In May of 2004, once again my family was notified that Kathy's case was going to be reopened. The last reopening was in 1983, twenty-one years earlier. How could so much time pass by since the last reopening? My family still waited for the day when we would be told the case had been solved and people had been charged.

Here we go again, gearing up for round three of reliving her brutal death. Her face appeared in the newspapers and on the local television stations, and the pain resurrected from deep within. The anxiety and fears of the awful night she didn't return home swirled around in my head. The visions of the events became vivid. I could see her face as she lay in the casket. The bruises on her neck, hands, and face that the mortician meticulously tried to hide with makeup flashed before my eyes. I heard his voice say to us, "Make sure you instruct people not to touch her. She's very fragile." I visualized the placement of her bangs to hide an injury underneath. After all these years, how could such things still be so vivid, so fresh in my mind?

I pleaded with God that day. "Don't let the investigators quit until they see results. They are vital in solving this mystery. Lead them, and give them wisdom."

Just when I thought my wounded heart was healing, a situation would come along to reopen the wound. Before I realized it, my heart would begin aching again. As I struggled to carry on, I looked for strength in places other than myself. My life included a strong faith in God. With Him, life's journey is difficult; without Him, it's almost unbearable.

CHAPTER THIRTY-EIGHT

The state police reopened the case and assigned a detective in Franklin to lead the investigation. This time it was a woman, which was a first for us. She began the tedious task of organizing the files from 1971. Once that was done, she did the same with all the files created from the 1983 reopening.

When Kathy's case was reopened in 1983, I was told by a friend of mine who worked for the state police that the files from the 1971 investigation consisted of stacks and stacks of boxes filled with documentation that had been collected. This detective had her hands full. I couldn't imagine the task of sorting through all of that paperwork and then proceeding to sift through the information that was collected from 1983.

After going through and organizing the documents from 1971 and 1983, she would then have to include anything that would come out in the 2004 investigation. I wondered if there would ever be enough information collected, enough files created, that someday produced results. Would this new reopening finally produce the results that my family had waited so long for? I didn't know that it would, but I did know that the pain of going over it all again never changed. It always caused the heart to ache and the eyes to weep. Hopefully this time someone will come forward with the crucial piece to the puzzle needed to put this case to rest.

My good friend Rich gave me this scripture in relation to Kathy's murder. When Cain slew his brother, Abel, the Lord said to him in Genesis 4:9–10, *And the Lord said unto Cain, "Where is Abel thy brother?" And he said, "I know not: Am I my brother's keeper?" And he said, "What hast thou done? The voice of thy brother's blood crieth unto me from the ground."* Just as Abel's voice cried up to God from the ground because his blood had been shed unjustly, so does Kathy's voice cry up to God from the ground because her blood was shed unjustly. It's been more than thirty years since she's cried up from the ground for justice, and I pray this time her voice will be heard.

I went to the cemetery and slowly made my way over to the ground where she lay. I wanted to tell her that she hadn't been forgotten. "Kathy, you know we'd do anything to make those involved in your murder pay for what they did. It's not right that all these years they've been able to walk free, while we were robbed of your presence.

"If we have to go through every detail and resurface every pain again, we will. We'll do whatever it takes, Kathy. Maybe this time it will be different; maybe this time we will finally see results from reliving the past. It's been so long since you've left us, and surely it's your time for justice. I love you, Kathy, and miss you very much." As

I turned away I said a little prayer. "God, give my family the strength they need to endure the anguish this reopening will bring. Give the people working on the case wisdom, and lead them in the way they need to go."

I reluctantly got into my car and put my head on the steering wheel; tears rolled down my cheeks. With a deep breath, I mentally tried to prepare for what was ahead.

In the past investigations, there were many questions asked but little knowledge shared with us. Being left in the dark was hard to cope with. We knew that the police could not share a lot of information with us, but that didn't make it easier. When not equipped with knowledge, it was hard to have hope. I wanted things to be different this time. I wanted justice for Kathy, and I didn't want the police to hold back in the investigation. If her remains needed to be exhumed for possible DNA, I wanted that; and so did my family. It had been suggested in 1983, but the investigators decided against it. Would they do it now?

I could only pray that maybe now the timing was right, and people who were afraid to come forward with information years ago would step up to the plate and do the right thing. I asked God to have His hand in this reopening and reveal new leads.

This time I want those investigating Kathy's case to remember what their badge stands for: to uphold the law and seek justice for those who cannot seek it for themselves. I want them to remember a young girl who was raped, beaten, strangled, and run over as if her life didn't matter at all. I am counting on them. Kathy is counting on them.

A poem dedicated to
Pat & Rich Kirby
Kris & Gretchen Brandenburg

BY KAREN BEAUDIN

Lord, heal my broken heart I pray.
Let nothing quench my love this day.
Let not the trials you have brought
Consume me and control my thoughts.

Through suffering, my eyes seek you.
Let glory come from skies of blue.
When showers seem to never end,
Remind me, Lord, You are my friend.

When waters all about me rise,
When flames reach up and cause me strife,
When in those times, I stand alone,
My heart yearns for heaven, my eternal home.

So as my heart weeps with these tears,
Hold it tenderly; calm my fears.
Your hand in mine, you walk beside
To lead me up this mountainside.

AUTHOR'S NOTE

A Child Is Missing covers the period of 1971 to 2003. In 2004, Kathy's case was reactivated for the second time, the first being in 1983. Because of the reopening, there has been an enormous amount of new information and activity on the case. It is for this reason I felt a sequel was needed to cover 2004 to the present day. The new book will is titled *A Child Is Missing: Searching for Justice*. My family has been searching for justice for years but with great urgency since 2004. Years are fleeting, and we are running out of time to convict the murderer and bring Kathy the justice she deserves.

In 2006, her remains were exhumed in hopes of obtaining DNA. Also in 2006, a man named Edward Dukette walked into a Florida police station and turned himself in, confessing he had killed Kathy and needed to be arrested. Later, he recanted and no arrest was made.

Kathy's murder has received local and national attention. WMUR of Manchester, Fox News in Boston, and CNN have all aired stories about her. On October 30, 2009, ABC's 20/20 did a story on Kathy called Vanished: Ghosts of Autumn Air. The attention on a national level brought in new leads and new information.

I and my family fought for the New Hampshire Cold Case Unit. At the present time there are over one hundred unsolved murders in New Hampshire. We spoke before the senate, telling them Kathy's story. We made it personal, holding posters and wearing T-shirts with Kathy's picture on them. The bill was passed, and the Cold Case Unit is now working on unsolved murders full time. My family may never see an arrest in Kathy's case, but it will happen for some other family, and we will rejoice with them. Our fight was not only for Kathy but for all those who still wait for justice.

I hope this book, *A Child Is Missing*, and the sequel, *A Child Is Missing: Searching For Justice*, will help bring in new leads and be a part of solving Kathy's murder.

For more information and updates on the progress being made in Kathy's murder investigation, go to www.kbeaudin.com

THANK YOU

I thank my Lord and Savior for allowing me to write this story; He led me all the way. Thanks to my three daughters: Joscelyn, Melissa, and Nicole. You are like freshly cut flowers in a delicate vase. Special thanks to Joscelyn, who still loves me even after all the photo work and computer questions. Melissa, you excel in how you love and take care of your family. My sweet grandchildren—Wyatt, Logan, and Tucker—you have made me laugh on days I never thought I could. Josh and Dan, thank you for loving my girls. Ann, Roger, and Janet, we have endured; I love you. Ann, I love that you're my big sister and Janet our little detective. As children, together we walked the path of pain and made it to the other side.

To the Beaudin family, I love you. Thanks, Mom, for encouraging me. My dearest friends, Rich and Pat, thank you for all you have done for me. I cherish your prayers and all those who pray for me and my family. Gretchen, you have arms that wrap around those in need. I love you, my dear friend. To my pastors, you have taught and guided me through my life. Special thanks to Pastor Leversee and Melanie; you are an example of God's love. Don and Janie, your kindness and love helped me through a very difficult time. Janie, you reminded me to always listen to God for direction. May God bless you both for your generosity. Robin, you are an encourager. JoAnne, your presence illuminates the love you have for God. Amanda, you are a good friend. God has a plan for you; stay faithful. Gordon, thank you for the newspaper articles and your interest in wanting this case solved. Tom, you have been a blessing to my family. Your desire to get the bad guy is evident when you speak. Jim, you went beyond the call of duty, and we are thankful. Bob and Jen, Fox News, Boston; your kindness during the interview meant so much to all of us. Your devotion to get the real story out is refreshing.

Thank you, ABC 20/20, for telling Kathy's story with compassion and accuracy. Donna, keep the faith. Thanks to all those in law enforcement who seek justice for the ones who cannot speak for themselves. Stephanie, you are one of them; thank you for your kindness. You wear your badge with honor and pride. Nicole, reach for your dream to be one of them.

At times there are some who lose sight of their purpose in life to uphold the law, but there are many that walk the road of justice. Lynda Cheldelin Fell, creator of Grief Diaries, you are an angel in disguise. You used your grief to help thousands facing their sorrow journey.

Finally, to those who feel they have lost their way in the sea of pain, keep looking; there is hope.

KAREN BEAUDIN

CONTACT

If you have any information about the murder

of Kathy Lynn Gloddy, please contact:

New Hampshire Cold Case Unit

New Hampshire Department of Justice

33 Capitol Street

Concord, NH 03301

Telephone: (603) 271-3658

Fax: (603) 271-2110

TDD Access: Relay NH 1-800-735-2964

www.doj.nh.gov/criminal/cold-case

ABOUT KAREN BEAUDIN

Karen Beaudin is an author and public speaker who addresses the subject of unsolved homicides to institutions including law enforcement and universities during training seminars, conferences, and criminal justice programs. Speaking engagements have included the Unsolved Homicide Training Course for the Bureau of Criminal Investigations in  Ohio and the keynote speaker at the 10th Annual National Missing Persons Conference in North Carolina. Karen's media interviews include Elizabeth Vargas from ABC 20/20, Bob Ward with Crime Reporter from Fox News Boston, and Sean MacDonald, Andy Hershberger, and Ray Brewer from WMUR TV. In 2009, Karen and her sisters were influential in establishing New Hampshire's first Cold Case Unit.

During Victims' Rights Week 2010, the Gloddy family received a certificate of appreciation from New Hampshire Governor John Lynch for their outstanding service on behalf of victims of crime. In 2012, the Ohio Attorney General recognized Karen for her advocacy in promoting cold case units. Also, the Fraternal Order of Police in Ohio recognized her for her valuable contribution to Ohio's law enforcement community and the Ohio Unsolved Homicides Initiative.

In loving memory of

Kathy Lynn Gloddy

PUBLISHED BY ALYBLUE MEDIA

www.AlyBlueMedia.com

Made in the USA
Middletown, DE
03 February 2018